Copyright

All rights reserved. Ian Moore asserts his right always to be identified as the author of this work. No part may be copied or transmitted without written permission from the publisher.

© Ian Moore 2023

First published by Lucius 2023

For more details and rights enquiries contact:
Lucius-ebooks@live.com

Cover design & illustration by Moira Kay Nicol
moirakaynicol.com

Dedication
Bill Booth, 1929-2022

The Lost Birds of *Middlemarch*, Britain and the World

Ian Moore

LUCIUS

CONTENTS

A personal note: Anoraks

Prologue: Flycatchers

Part I: Middlemarch
A birdwatching walk through the 1970s
Actual days out
The list

Part II: The Norfolk Years
The Wren-Pipit
North Norfolk

Part III: Corstorphine Hill
Déjà vu

Epilogue
Triumph or illusion?

Appendices
The data
About the author
Index
Notes

A PERSONAL NOTE

From a young age I had always wanted to be an author; I just didn't think it would take fifty years to write a book. Now, I feel I owe it to my anoraky 11-year-old self not to let these statistics gather dust. When I embarked on a meticulous journey of recording all the birds I would spot, I'm sure I did harbour an inkling that it was something more than a private account, a vanity project. For here is a unique and true record, one fine strand of Britain's natural heritage, a thread that permeates the faded wildlife tapestry of the past five decades. And if it can play a small role in helping wildlife and those of us who hold nature close to our hearts, then it will have been worthwhile, all these years of vigilant observation, diligent note-taking and determined counting.

Ian Moore
Edinburgh
24 March, 2023

A graphic representation of 88% decline

PROLOGUE

QUESTION: why are car windscreens and motorbike helmets no longer splattered with insects? In the good old days of the Triumph Herald and the BSA Bantam it was an occupational hazard to make pit stops to scrape away the sticky smears. At times it could be akin to driving through a hailstorm. I remember, on my motorcycle at night, it was foolhardy to ride without a visor and a scarf; larger moths could feel like minor meteor strikes.

I have some possible explanations:

A) Technological streamlining of modern modes of transport.
B) Natural selection favouring insects that fly higher than the average vehicle.
C) An explosion in the population of the Spotted Flycatcher.

Two of these choices are possible, if improbable in varying degrees. One is patently false. However, most folk are not birdwatchers, and the incorrect answer may not be immediately apparent.

Most folk, however, are motorists – and among those old enough to remember the 1970s, I detect a sense of nostalgia for those troublesome splats. Perhaps their loss connects, subliminally, unconsciously – discomfortingly, even – to a more profound folk memory, of the way things were.

PART I
THE 1970s
'MIDDLEMARCH'

Watling Street barn, pre-1831-1978

'MIDDLEMARCH'

Between 1970 and the autumn of 1977, when I left my Midlands home for St Andrews University on the east coast of Scotland, I recorded 522 birdwatching walks on my local patch. I meticulously noted every bird I saw or heard, by species and numbers. On 23rd April 1972 it was 86 Linnets, 46 Goldfinches, 17 Tree Sparrows, 17 Yellowhammers and 13 Skylarks (and 24 species in total). I was so keen that on 21st December 1971 I went out 3 times!

I spent my formative years living in Burbage, today a suburb of Hinckley, but still in the 1960s and early 1970s a village community that was comparatively little changed over many generations.

Especially on the south side, where we lived, fields were never far away, and an apron of market gardens, nurseries, orchards and allotments provided a gradual delineation into the surrounding farmland. There were few if any absolutely wild places, but low-intensity of land use gave to the countryside a depth that is entirely alien to today's cosmetic façade.

I grew up with several friends who were farmers' sons, and laboured at haymaking and potato picking. During and after the war my great-grandfather George Gretton had farmed the Outwoods near Burbage Common. (As an aside he once arrested a downed German airman at the points of a pitchfork; when the Home Guard arrived at the farmhouse to take him into custody, the fellow surrendered from inside his flying jacket a fully loaded Luger!)

My own inclination from the earliest age was to escape through the palings and immerse myself in the human-hewn landscape that lay beyond. Like many small boys I cut my teeth on collections of great crested newts and short-tailed voles and butterflies and moths and their incredible larvae and – yes – even collecting birds' eggs numbered among the standard hobbies of village lads, alongside playing conkers, letting off bangers, and scrumping apples.

But I graduated under the wise mentorship of Mr Sherwood, my headmaster at Burbage Junior School, to emerge by the age of eleven a fully fledged and conscientious birdwatcher. I joined the YOC – the Young Ornithologists' Club (then the junior arm of the RSPB) and got my first mention in the 'Special Notes' section of the Apr-Jun 1970 edition of the magazine 'Bird Life'.

However it took me three years of trying before I actually had a submission published in full: an account of a Robin bathing in the raindrops trapped in the hawthorn hedge in my Grandmother's garden.

Middlemarch

Like probably half the local population I was born in the nearby George Eliot Hospital, named after our most famous daughter. *Middlemarch* thus being required reading, I have often wondered, where the heck is it? A work of fiction and no clear indication – was the imaginary market town based upon Nuneaton, or perhaps Hinckley? My fellow Midlander Mary Anne Evans would have visited both. That she hailed from farming stock in this very area, reading between the lines of her eponymous novel it seems to me, the town aside, the book is surely set in the agricultural lands that straddle the Warwickshire-Leicestershire border, and which exactly one century after publication corresponded to my local patch. The novel's many insights into Victorian agrarian life give a sense of what the countryside was like – and that it was not so different from my time.

For the purposes of this narrative – and indeed to accurately represent how I went about my business – my local patch comprised three components, juxtaposed – two areas where I birdwatched intensively and, in between, the greater expanse of farmland that linked them.

I am a little embarrassed by the prosaic names I gave to these places (and to the rather wooden descriptions of some of my sightings); no one reading my logbooks would guess that here was a boy destined for a career as an advertising copywriter.

The sites, as follows:

1. 'Usual Area'

Across the street and through my Grandmother's garden was a rough trapezium of 50 acres enclosed by (clockwise) Sketchley Road, where I lived, Cotes Road, Coventry Road and Wolvey Road. This was made up of a large agricultural field (half the total area), rough paddocks and rank grassland, and partially abandoned orchards and allotments. I could pop out here any time I had a spare half-hour.

2. 'Fields south of Coventry Road'

This was more of a thoroughfare than a destination, the farmland that lay between the south side of Burbage and the Roman Watling Street, roughly bisected by Bullfurlong Lane, in those days an unmetalled track that formed the principal public right of way through the locality. From Coventry Road to the Watling Street, a walk due south of just under a mile, through an area of something like 520 acres within viewing range, typically took half an hour, although it could be extended by diversions en route, flocking birds perhaps, or several small ponds that were often of interest.

3. 'Area of Foster's Pond'

The 'Fields south of Coventry Road' took me to the county boundary, the aforementioned Watling Street. More or less immediately upon crossing from Leicestershire into

Warwickshire, I would reach an interesting arrangement of lake (Foster's Pond), stream, marsh, woods, smaller ponds and farmland that could be accessed by a public footpath that continued on towards Wolvey, but which was rarely trodden by locals. This area covered approximately 177 acres, of which 41 were woodland. A full birdwatching walk, there and back, would take me a whole morning. As I grew older I was able to access the area by bike and motorbike and even my first old banger of a car. Such means of approach became necessary when the M69 cut a swathe of tarmac through my cherished route in 1976-77.

So, these three components make up the patch for which I have borrowed the title *Middlemarch*. That it spans two counties lies at the root of this naming conundrum – clearly it is neither West nor East Midlands; Warwickshire belonging to the former and Leicestershire to the latter. *Middle* seems apposite. I recall that childhood trips to the seaside in any direction seemed to take forever, notwithstanding the single-carriageway trunk roads and a 48 bhp Morris Minor. We were unequivocally in the middle … and *march* is certainly what I did, day upon day, year upon year!

On a scale of one-to-five

The interesting thing about my perception of my local patch – almost ludicrous with hindsight – is how poorly I rated it on my own scale of 'Good for Birds'.

I suppose the start point for this perception was that the general area looked quite nondescript. There was neither the rolling landscape of East Leicestershire, nor the lush countryside of South Warwickshire. By comparison, here it felt like something of a no-man's land, bereft of hills or water, or even a small nature reserve that might attract birdwatchers from beyond.

I also harboured a sneaking impression that England, more broadly, was not the place it used to be. Were there not once wild areas of marsh and fen and forest, and heaths and commons where the birds I knew to be on the verge of extinction could be found? Time and again I had devoured a favourite book – *All About Wild Life* by Reginald Harrison, Collins (1942) – the captivating adventures of bosom pals and boy naturalists, Ted and Jim, under the tutelage of village stalwart old Doctor Woodward. They went sugaring for moths, created a home-made aquarium, built a cage to rear larvae. After watching badgers, there was this exchange (quoted verbatim):

"Good-night, Ted. See you to-morrow. And we'll take a walk up to Curlew Common on Saturday afternoon if it's fine. Don't forget to bring the field glasses with you, and we'll do some bird-stalking up there."

"Right-ho ! and good-night, Jim. Remember to make a note of the badgers in your diary."

And they found the birds that I dreamed of seeing, the likes of Red-backed Shrike, Nightjar and Woodlark.

My perception of there having been 'the good old days' was bolstered by a sheaf of ornithological notes that were given to me by Ted Thornhill, village postmaster and Chairman of Hinckley & District Natural History Society, which I was later to join. These original pages, penned in flowing longhand in traditional style, are a contemporary account of the Great Pallas's Sandgrouse Invasion of 1888, the culmination of two decades' irruptive behaviour. It seems even *Middlemarch* received its share of this exotic and most enigmatic species.

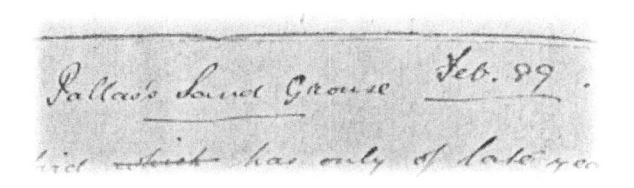

Organised trips with the local natural history society had also begun to open my eyes to the concept that there were places that were 'Good for Birds'. These ranged from Eye Brook Reservoir (35 miles across in Rutland), to the Mecca for all birdwatchers, Cley Marshes in Norfolk (130 miles). Eye-opening though these experiences were, they only served to reinforce my impression that my local patch was quite ordinary.

I imagine if I were pressed at the time, I would have invented a grading system along roughly these lines:

    5 star – "Excellent" – **Cley Marshes**
    4 star – "Above average" – **Eye Brook Reservoir**
    3 star – "Average" – **Area of Foster's Pond**
    2 star – "Below average" – **Usual Area**
    1 star – "Poor" – **Fields south of Coventry Road**

Log books

From the very beginning I had a strong sense that I needed to keep a log book. I had read extensively about how to be a birdwatcher. And it appealed to an obsessive nature that I thought was quite normal.

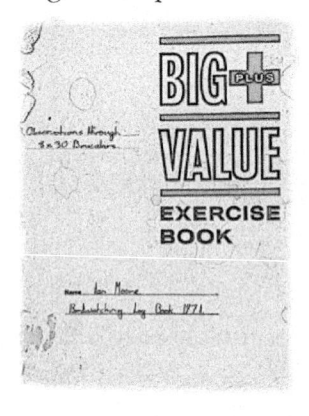

My now-precious collection of log books begins with a flimsy yellowed jotter, 'Big Plus Value Exercise Book', which despite being made with the cheapest paper is reassuringly marked 'British Manufacture'. On the back cover are 'Arithmetical Tables' that include 'Hay and Straw Weight' (always handy to know that 36lb of straw or 56lb of old hay equals a truss) and 'Imperial Heaped Measure' (8 gallons being a bushel, and 3 bushels a sack). Some allusion to *Middlemarch* here, methinks.

On the front I have written with a fountain pen:

Observations through 8x30 binoculars
Birdwatching log book 1971

It seems this was a book of short narratives, rather than the detailed lists of species and numbers that my records would soon become.

There are entries headed:

Robin's courtship display, February 23rd
Unusual garden visitor, March 14th
Mobbing of owl, April 4th

Delving into the detail, here is a short example from my Usual Area, dated 22nd April 1971:

The ploughed field is now occupied by a large flock of Linnets. Around Nov-Dev 1970 it was the feeding ground of several charms of Goldfinches and flocks of House and Tree Sparrows. These birds gradually dispersed, leaving small groups of Gold, Green and Chaffinches. After the finches came Skylarks (Jan-Feb), but as spring and warmer weather approached they split up from the flocks.

Between 19th-26th August 1971 I attended a YOC course, based at a youth hostel on the Isle of Man. This professionalised my approach to note-taking, and by now I was producing detailed lists and counts for every visit I made. Here is one example, dated 23rd December 1971:

Time from 9.25 a.m., cloudy, wind force 0-1, has rained:

Woodpigeon 2
Skylark 19
Meadow Pipit 2
Wren 1
Dunnock 3
Robin 1
Blackbird 13

Song Thrush 1
Mistle Thrush 1
Willow Tit 1 – recognised by pale wing patch and sooty cap
Blue Tit 2
Great Tit 1
Reed Bunting 7
Chaffinch 1 pair
Greenfinch 4
Goldfinch 2
Bullfinch 1 female
House Sparrow 24
Tree Sparrow 12
Starling 40
Magpie 2
Rook 13

The ornithologist reading this might just feel the first inkling of what is to come. While it is a modest list of 22 species, an hour's snapshot on a dreary December morning, matter-of-factly reported are several entries that would raise an eyebrow were these notes made today.

Please join with me on a stroll through those old times.

A BIRDWATCHING WALK THROUGH THE 1970s

And so, a wander through my old stamping ground – the vicarious experience I have relived in sifting through my log books. What follows is a compilation of seasons and years. Inevitably there was some ebb and flow in the species and numbers that were present. I would never see or hear every available bird on a single walk – and naturally there were no Cuckoos, for example, in winter and no Fieldfares in summer. But broadly speaking, this account represents the bird population of *Middlemarch* in the 1970s, residents, summer and winter visitors, and transient species of various grades, some migratory and others just passing more locally.

As you kindly accompany me on this journey, I would just ask that you keep in mind my star-rating system.

STAGE 1: 'USUAL AREA'

I would have woken to the irrepressible chirrup of **House Sparrows**, the most abundant species on my patch.

It appears on almost every single one of my 522 recorded walks, with flocks of up to 230 in my Usual Area. Like many birds, they reached their numerical peak at the end of the breeding season, in September and October, and gradually declined through natural attrition to begin again in spring.

HOUSE SPARROW
17.7 million pairs in 1970s
5.3 million pairs in 2020s
70% decline

Before ducking under the strap of my prized Christmas present of 1971, my East German Carl Zeiss 10x50 binoculars, and slipping the Observer's Book of Birds and a notebook into my cotton webbing haversack, I would begin with a glance out of my bedroom window. The view was north, towards Hinckley; the silhouette of St Mary's church pricking the horizon, a mile away.

Across the fields a pair of **Carrion Crows** regularly nested, high in a steepling elm, and could be seen flighting back and forth with twigs and, later, food. One small detail thrown up by my records is that this species was less numerous than I would have remembered – the most I ever recorded was 11 on a single outing, and that a full walk to the Area of Foster's Pond.

Leaving our back gate, I would cross Sketchley Road into my Grandmother's garden, diagonally opposite. In the traditional village style the long narrow plot stretched back for some 75 yards, and a shallow ditch ran down the left-hand side. Silted up and overgrown with watercress, this was a field drain that exists to this day (much culverted) as a tributary to Sketchley Brook, which gave the street that divides Burbage from Hinckley its name of Brookside.

The next bird I hoped to see was not to be expected in a village garden. From time to time in winter, a **Common Snipe** would explode with a shriek from the stream. Always a propitious start to my walk.

COMMON SNIPE
400,000 pairs in 1970s
80,000 pairs in 2020s
80% decline

If I was really lucky, I could add a **Grey Heron** passing overhead; more excitement, the largest bird regularly to grace the local skies, their seemingly purposeful movements an enjoyable little mystery.

GREY HERON
15,900 pairs in 1970s
13,000 pairs in 2020s
18% decline

On the wing in summer there were always **Swifts**, **Swallows** and **House Martins**. **Swifts** (usually up to about 10, but as many as 30 by the end of the season) I always associated with Burbage church, a mile to the east, where I believe they bred.

SWIFT
140,000 pairs in 1990s
59,000 pairs in 2020s
58% decline

There was a regular small colony of **House Martins** that nested on the Co-op building just along Sketchley Road; these were also typically around the dozen mark, with up to 30 noted in August.

HOUSE MARTIN
637,000 pairs in 1990s
510,000 pairs in 2020s
20% decline

Likewise, **Swallows** were present in small numbers, breeding for instance in the horses' sheds close by; a peak of 80 passed through my Usual Area on 23.9.72.

SWALLOW
1,012,000 pairs in 1970s
860,000 pairs in 2020s
15% decline

The bottom half of my Grandmother's garden was adjoined on the left by the first of two rough paddocks in which ponies were kept. Alongside the ditch grew a row of English elms, with some hawthorn, providing cover for birds, and at the very end a cluster of sycamores around a small lifeless pool that was part of the brook drainage system.

When Dutch elm disease struck, for a couple of weeks in February 1972 there was an agonising silver lining, for both **Great Spotted Woodpeckers** and **Lesser Spotted Woodpeckers** were ever-present, busily depleting the dead and dying trees of their easily peeled bark for the *Scolytus* beetle pupae beneath.

LESSER SPOTTED WOODPECKER
15,000 pairs in 1970s
1,500 pairs in 2020s
90% decline

I would always stop to scan the nearest paddock through my binoculars. The ground was rich in dung, and horse flies and wild flowers were abundant; at night scores of ghost swift moths would hover eerily in their courtship displays. Most common here were **Starlings** feeding avariciously, but in spring **Yellow Wagtails** would arrive to breed in the vicinity, typically a single pair. The area beside a stretch of the brook at which the horses drank was particularly attractive for them.

YELLOW WAGTAIL
47,000 pairs in 1970s
15,000 pairs in 2020s
68% decline

Starlings were ubiquitous, breeding locally in small numbers, often in rooftops; with as many as 275 recorded feeding in my Usual Area in December, and up to 500 on my extended walk. On 26.12.74. an estimated 10,000 flew over my Usual Area at dusk.

STARLING
10 million pairs in 1970s
1.8 million pairs in 2020s
82% decline

Another bird that would have announced itself by this point was the **Cuckoo**. I took for granted that it would appear at the end of April; its call was as much a part of village life as the sound of the church bells from St Catherine's on a Sunday morning.

Here is a direct quote from my log book; I was aged 12:

14 Aug 1971

"The juvenile Cuckoo, which has been seen for five consecutive days, was seen in the horses' field, being annoyed by a perky cock Yellow Wagtail. It chased the wagtail from post to post and suddenly shot off in pursuit of it across the field. The wagtail evaded the acrobatic cuckoo, which flew away as if in disgust."

CUCKOO
38,000 pairs in 1970s
18,000 pairs in 2020s
53% decline

The paddocks were also attractive to migrant species, passing through mainly in early autumn, August and September, stopping off to feed upon invertebrates, perching on the posts that supported the perimeter barbed wire, or the hedgerow that bordered the west side of both fields. Three species were annual visitors: **Redstart, Whinchat** and **Wheatear**.

WHINCHAT
109,000 pairs in 1990s
47,000 pairs in 2020s
57% decline

I suspect that these passage migrants were British birds, making their way east and south from breeding territories in Wales and the Pennines. Later I would come to experience 'drift migrants', continental birds that could appear in great 'falls' on Britain's east coast.

But while I only ever saw a handful on my local patch – two or three of each species per year, and generally several **Whinchats** – there was always that added sense of anticipation that something unexpected might turn up. On a single walk on 31.8.75. I recorded one of each of these three birds.

Moreover, there were other migrants – such as a **Pied Flycatcher** (11.9.71.), a superb male **Black Redstart** (29.9.72.), and several late October sightings of **Stonechats**, including a pair on 24.10.75. I had one single sighting of a **Lesser Whitethroat**, an autumn passage bird.

PIED FLYCATCHER
30,000 pairs in 1990s
17,000 pairs in 2020s
43% decline

But I am still not out of my Grandmother's garden – and it was here that I found my first ever **Goldcrest** (14.3.71) – as memorable a moment for an 11-year-old novice birdwatcher as many of the rare and exotic species I have discovered since. There is nothing quite like reading about a bird, wishing to see it … and one day the exhilaration of identifying it for oneself.

I grew to appreciate that there were **Goldcrests** in small numbers throughout my patch, despite an almost complete absence of conifers. I do, however, recall finding a **Goldcrest's** tiny nest slung beneath the branch of a yew in Aston Flamville churchyard, a couple of miles away.

GOLDCREST
744,000 pairs in 1970s
610,000 pairs in 2020s
18% decline

Also frequenting the area of adjoining, extensive and largely unkempt gardens, would be the likes of **Marsh Tit**, often as a pair – this latter species being particularly vocal and easy to locate, and widespread throughout the district. They would visit garden feeders with other tits. My notes show up to 6 **Marsh Tits** recorded on a single walk.

MARSH TIT
1.6 million pairs in 1970s
410,000 pairs in 2020s
75% decline

My escape route from my Grandmother's garden involved a small amount of scrambling to leap the ditch and then cross back on shoogly planks half-submerged in the black pool behind the horses' sheds, thence to force my way through the hedgerow into a corner of the large arable field that was part of Cross Roads Farm. At 25 acres it constituted the largest single unit of my Usual Area. It was separated on its east side from the paddocks by a thick hedge, and bounded by Wolvey Road to the west.

This field invariably held birds, often in large numbers, and one of my earliest records is from a tiny notebook that pre-dates my first more formal log book (and referenced above), of a charm of 50 **Goldfinches** that were feeding on 'daisy heads' in late October 1970. The plant was likely mayweed, an abundant field weed and popular with seed-eaters.

KESTREL
88,000 pairs in 1970s
46,000 pairs in 2020s
48% decline

Kestrels were seemingly ever-present, almost as though there was a kite or two tethered to a string above the field in the role of scarecrow. This was an iconic bird for a small boy – not least because I strongly identified with my fictional contemporary, Billy Casper. (Ken Loach's epic film *Kes* had been released in 1969.) Indeed, as people in the village got to know me as the 'Bird Boy', I would from time to time be brought injured birds to look after. Like I would know what to do! On one occasion I was presented with a young Kestrel – but unlike Billy, I successfully released it back into the wild – literally in the nick of time, because word had got round and a local gang came knocking on my door. I was able to point out the creature in a nearby treetop and leave them trying to coax it down.

My respect for this feisty little falcon was only enhanced when it put a talon right through my fingernail and out the other side! These days I have some involvement in an assisted Kestrel breeding project, and am more judicious.

Linnets nested prolifically in the mainly hawthorn and elder hedgerows bordering the big field, and there was an ebb and flow, year-round, of mixed flocks of sparrows, finches, buntings, larks and pipits.

LINNET
977,000 pairs in 1970s
430,000 pairs in 2020s
56% decline

Linnet numbers could reach 100, **Tree Sparrows** were widespread (even nesting in a box in my Grandmother's garden), typically around 10 or so but as many as 80 in my Usual Area, often flocking together with **House Sparrows**.

TREE SPARROW
2 million pairs in 1970s
200,000 pairs in 2020s
90% decline

Greenfinches, as well as being a regular garden visitor, would also feed on the stubble and field weed seeds, with up to 25 noted in my Usual Area.

GREENFINCH
4.7 million pairs in 1970s
1.7 million pairs in 2020s
64% decline

Reed Buntings were present in small numbers throughout the walk, although with up to 60 recorded just in my Usual Area on 1.12.73. They are not thought of as a flocking bird, but would often intermingle with similar-looking sparrows.

REED BUNTING
347,000 pairs in 1970s
250,000 pairs in 2020s
28% decline

Yellowhammer, too, was a regular with up to 20 noted in my Usual Area.

YELLOWHAMMER
1.8 million pairs in 1970s
700,000 pairs in 2020s
60% decline

Small numbers of **Corn Buntings** also bred here, favouring the telegraph wires alongside Wolvey Road for their song perches, their creaky voice a contrast to their sweeter sounding and more colourful cousin.

CORN BUNTING
100,000 pairs in 1970s
11,000 pairs in 2020s
89% decline

Four of the year-round species in the big field were **Skylark, Rook, Grey Partridge** and **Pied Wagtail**. Several pairs of **Skylarks** nested in the rough grassland around the orchards and their airborne song was an all-pervasive accompaniment to my walks during spring and early summer. Numbers would build up in winter with a maximum recorded in my Usual Area of 53 on 25.11.72.

SKYLARK
3.4 million pairs in 1970s
1.5 million pairs in 2020s
56% decline

Rooks, too, were ever present. There was a rookery just a quarter of a mile away near the Three Pots roundabout, and usually some of these birds feeding on my patch – reaching a peak of 250 on 28.10.73. **Grey Partridge** bred in small numbers, with a maximum of 5 noted.

GREY PARTRIDGE
529,000 pairs in 1970s
37,000 pairs in 2020s
93% decline

Pied Wagtails were often present, usually in ones and twos. I add **Grey Wagtail** in at this point, but with just a couple of sightings, 3 on 21.9.72 and another on 19.10.74.

GREY WAGTAIL
69,000 pairs in 1970s
38,000 pairs in 2020s
45% decline

As the year progressed beyond the breeding season, substantial numbers of a variety of species would build up in Cross Roads Farm field. Their nature and type could vary according to the land use, which might be cereal and thence winter stubble, or crops that ranged from peas to mangolds. Moreover, these were the days of traditional practices, and there was always a large 'weed' component, and no doubt a healthy invertebrate population that was attractive for birds. I have mentioned that **Skylarks** increased from a few breeding pairs up to over 50 in winter, and these were joined between September and May by **Meadow Pipits**, peaking at 16 in my Usual Area on 18.11.72.

MEADOW PIPIT
3.2 million pairs in 1970s
2 million pairs in 2020s
37% decline

Lapwing, likewise, while present year-round in the wider patch, would appear in the big field in tandem with **Meadow Pipit** timings, and a recorded maximum of 200 on 16.10.71.

LAPWING
270,000 pairs in 1970s
97,500 pairs in 2020s
64% decline

Despite being just about as far inland as it is possible to get in Britain, small numbers of gulls were a regular feature of my walks. The network of Midlands reservoirs provided safe roosting sites, and the farmland a reliable source of food. Between May and September, there could be occasional sightings of a handful of **Lesser Black-backed Gulls**, while a maximum of 60 was recorded passing over my Usual Area on 30.3.73. Most gulls appeared outside the breeding season. The highest totals for the other species were: 4 **Great Black-backed Gulls**, 19 **Herring Gulls**, 23 **Black-headed Gulls**, and 4 **Common Gulls**.

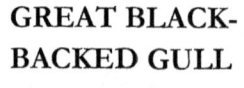

GREAT BLACK-BACKED GULL
29,000 pairs in 1970s
17,000 pairs in 2020s
42% decline

HERRING GULL
286,000 pairs in 1970s
140,000 pairs in 2020s
51% decline

Back to passerines, and thrushes were also a winter feature of my Usual Area, with all 5 species in evidence. **Blackbird**, **Song Thrush** and **Mistle Thrush** were of course present all year, the latter usually just a pair, but up to 6 on occasion.

MISTLE THRUSH
395,000 pairs in 1970s
170,000 pairs in 2020s
57% decline

The big field could be a good place to see them, but the reliable attraction was the permanent horses' paddock nearest to my Grandmother's garden. Here, 23 **Blackbirds** and 9 **Song Thrushes** were noted in February 1972, and 35 **Fieldfares** in December 1971.

SONG THRUSH
2.4 million pairs in 1970s
1.2 million pairs in 2020s
49% decline

As many as 85 **Fieldfares** were recorded during October 1972, and a maximum of 10 **Redwings**. In general, **Fieldfares** outnumbered **Redwings** by more than two-to-one on my overall patch during the 1970s.

BLACKBIRD
6 million pairs in 1970s
5.1 million pairs in 2020s
15% decline

From Cross Roads Farm field I would normally cut across between the two paddocks to the other main area of habitat interest. Lying to the east of the paddocks and extending beyond the rough track known as Pyeharps, all the way to the unmetalled lane that was Cotes Road were about 15 acres of rough grassland and largely abandoned mature orchards interspersed with sporadically tended allotments. There were stands of rosebay willowherb, great bushes of brambles and patches of nettles. It was a run-to-ruin area attractive for wildlife and small hungry village boys.

The upper paddock (the most southerly of the two) was more often overgrown, rank grassland really – but it was good for **Skylarks** nesting and small mammals (so **Kestrels** often hunted over here), but one of my most vivid memories is of coming across a **Cuckoo** in the grass. I just stooped down and scooped it up! My first reaction was that it was injured – but when I held it aloft it flew away perfectly well. On reflection I think I perhaps saved a pair of Skylarks from the ignominy of foster parenthood.

That my first instinct was simply to pick up the bird might seem odd, but I was used to handling wildlife. These overgrown fields teemed with short-tailed voles and common shrews that made their woven grass nests under windblown sheets of corrugated iron from a contractor's barn that stood nearby – as smaller boys we used catch them for fun. I remember taking into junior school an injured common shrew that I had rescued from Tom, my tabby cat. This was a great entertainment for the class – we put in an empty aquarium and a dinner lady supplied a juicy chunk of red beef that soon revived it!

BULLFINCH
306,000 pairs in 1970s
190,000 pairs in 2020s
38% decline

The orchards attracted a wide variety of species, but of those I have not yet mentioned, notable were **Bullfinches**, which were birds I typically saw most days, but there was an obvious magnet in the fruit trees, and I have a record of

10 on 18.11.72. – a couple of family groups joined up, perhaps.

Spotted Flycatcher bred in the orchards, nesting I suspect in one of the many dilapidated sheds that also housed **Robins** and **Swallows**. I have a note of 2 adult **Spotted Flycatchers** feeding 2 juveniles in the orchards on 14.7.74. and this summer visitor was supplemented by passage migrants, often in early September.

SPOTTED FLYCATCHER
300,000 pairs in 1970s
36,000 pairs in 2020s
88% decline

But the special attraction for me of the orchards were the warblers. Here bred **Willow Warbler, Whitethroat, Grasshopper Warbler** and **Sedge Warbler**.

When I first discovered there were **Grasshopper Warblers**, I initially ignored the singing male. My pals and I had a regular cycling challenge, it was called "Doing a Pyeharps" – the idea being to pedal frantically along Coventry Road and slew into Pyeharps Road (then an unmetalled track with muddy ruts and huge puddles), and thence freewheel all the way to Sketchley Road on the slightest of downslopes.

My first **Grasshopper Warbler** I passed off as someone on a bike doing this very thing! It was made more authentic an explanation by the way the bird turns its head when singing, giving the impression of a bike approaching and then passing, a small Doppler effect.

GRASSHOPPER WARBLER
25,000 pairs in 1970s
12,000 pairs in 2020s
52% decline

Sedge Warblers seemed to thrive in the overgrown orchards, despite the ground here being very dry, and not what I would have considered their natural habitat. There were some invasive clumps of willows among the fruit trees, and the extensive brambles provided additional protective cover and food for all of the warblers.

SEDGE WARBLER
531,000 pairs in 1970s
260,000 pairs in 2020s
51% decline

If I was sticking to my Usual Area (something I did less as I grew older and felt more able to venture further afield) I would duck under the barbed wire into the lower paddock from which, behind the horses' sheds there was a secret way back into my Grandmother's garden.

There are species I have not hitherto mentioned that were regulars in my Usual Area – probably noted on almost every walk (as, of course, were many of the above). These are birds that were both garden-friendly and found in the fields, hedgerows and woodland beyond. They would include the following: **Blue Tit, Chaffinch, Coal Tit, Dunnock, Great Tit, Jackdaw, Magpie, Robin, Woodpigeon, Wren**.

DUNNOCK
3.4 million pairs in 1970s
2.3 million pairs in 2020s
33% decline

So that is my 'Usual Area'. Thus far I have logged 60 species as my cumulative list – the best I can see from my notes is about 35 species in a single day. Not bad, on reflection, for an area that I rated as: 2 star – "Below average".

STAGE 2: 'FIELDS SOUTH OF COVENTRY ROAD'

Between my two main birdwatching sites was the patch of farmland that I usually referred to in my log books as 'Fields south of Coventry Road'. At its greatest extent this was a considerable area (as I have mentioned, over 500 acres), really everything between the east-west extremities of Burbage, south to the Watling Street. But I was marching from A to B, from my Usual Area to the Area of Foster's Pond, and so I generally followed a direct route south using the public rights of way.

This would take me from Cross Roads Farm field, over Coventry Road, through three fields to meet up with Bullfurlong Lane, and onwards down tracks to Rowe's Farm. Husbanded by my classmate Peter's dad, it was a place I frequented as a youngster, and whence hailed my first dog, *Lady*, a loveable 'Heinz 57' mongrel.

This extended area was familiar to me in part through this farming connection, but also simply as one of the village boys that roamed everywhere and anywhere during our formative years – an innate drive to explore every pond and stream, every derelict or abandoned farm building or allotment or orchard; to peer with trepidation into every bottomless well; to climb with growing butterflies every swaying tree. It was the time of one's life.

And so, back to the birds.

Crossing Coventry Road, the first field held two ponds – the Twin Ponds – at a corner where three fields met, and thus provided a source of water for cattle in more than one enclosure. These days, ponds are few and far between, but they were a common feature of our locality, and I can recall at least a dozen that we as kids would visit to catch amphibians. Most famous was Record's Pond near Burbage Wood, accessed from Sapcote Road, which teemed with great crested and smooth newts.

Every pond had its nesting **Moorhens**, and attracted birds to drink. I recall once fishing a **Swallow** out of

Record's Pond with my beanpole-handled newting net – it misjudged a sortie to drink and crash-landed, and I don't think would have made it out, were it not for my intervention.

There were 8 ponds on my route down to the Area of Foster's Pond – and I have a record of as many as 50 Moorhens on a single walk (albeit the majority gathering to feed on the banks of Foster's Pond itself).

MOORHEN
313,000 pairs in 1970s
210,000 pairs in 2020s
33% decline

Another bird that would now begin to appear that did not frequent my Usual Area was **Pheasant**. Since it is a 'cultivated' bird, with roughly 50 million put down each year, it is not one that can be assessed for population trends. Nonetheless, it was a colourful and seemingly complementary addition to the countryside – the explosive call of the cock in spring woodland never failed to set the pulse racing. It was the next best thing to a Capercaillie!

Virtually all of the fields were bordered by dense high hedges, predominantly hawthorn, interspersed by tall English elms. They provided food, shelter and nesting sites for many birds. Indeed, the single square mile of farmland between Burbage and the Watling Street comprised over 80 fields, on average a size of just 6 acres per field. From a bird's-eye view it would have seemed like a kind of scrub-woodland latticework laid like a web over the countryside, and providing by my rough estimate over 20 miles of luxuriant hedgerow.

Comparing the map of my era to today's Google version, I can see that most of these fields have been replaced by 'developments' that are still expanding; the high hedgerows, of course, began to disappear at a much earlier date.

More of that later.

Sticking with the subject of fields, immediately past the Twin Ponds the footpath now led into one of my favourite pastures green. Small, narrow in fact, and high hedged with predominantly hawthorn, this was a perennial hay meadow, and in June and July *Lady* would surf the cool long grasses, sending up clouds of pollen and swarms of meadow browns.

It was in the hedgerow surrounding this meadow that I discovered my first flock of **Long-tailed Tits.** As with my first **Goldcrest**, it is one of my most treasured early birdwatching memories, those diminutive balls of pink-and-white-and-black candy floss on their stick tails.

TURTLE DOVE
180,000 pairs in 1970s
3,600 pairs in 2020s
98% decline

The same hedgerow was also a regular nesting site for **Turtle Dove**, the singing male flooding the resonant arena in late spring with a soothing somnambulistic purr that made you want to lie down and gaze at the blue heavens as golden brimstone butterflies fluttered by.

While the Fields South of Coventry Road held few birds that I considered 'specialities' (although who wouldn't want to hear that **Turtle Dove**?), what most strikes me, analysing my records, is that if my Usual Area was impressive by today's standards for its remarkable diversity, the adjacent farmland was noteworthy for its sheer abundance of birds, a feature which at the time I took entirely for granted.

Reading through my records rekindled faded memories of passerine flocks that rose and fell like waves breaking over late-summer cornfields and winter stubble. For example, on 2.9.73. there were 850 **House Sparrows** in a cereal crop alongside Bullfurlong Lane.

In January/February 1974 in the same vicinity there were combined flocks of **Tree Sparrow** (100), **Greenfinch** (120) and **Linnet** (40). On another occasion (23.11.75), just north of the Watling Street, a flock of 150 **Tree Sparrows** and 100 **Greenfinches**. By early January 1976 this flock reached an estimated 1000 birds, comprising **Greenfinch**, **Linnet**, **House Sparrow** and **Tree Sparrow** in roughly equal numbers. At earlier dates, here on 23.4.72., 46 **Goldfinches** and 30 **Linnets**, having already counted 56 **Linnets** in my Usual Area. And again on 21.1.73., 60 **Yellowhammers** and 20 **Reed Buntings**. A gathering of **Pied Wagtails** peaked at 70 on 23.3.76.

The full walk, in winter, could also deliver large numbers of thrushes. A flock of around 200 **Fieldfares** regularly frequented the fields close to the Foster's Pond woods – most likely seen in November and December, along with up to 100 **Redwings** (23.11.75. when 100 **Fieldfares** were also present). The resident thrushes at this time of year could also be prolific, with records of 15 **Mistle Thrushes**, 22 **Song Thrushes** and 60 **Blackbirds**.

The two large arable fields on the north side of the Watling Street and bisected by Soar Brook could host particularly impressive flocks. Coveys of **Grey Partridge** reached 30 on one occasion, and other species that would commonly gather to feed included **Collared Dove** (60), **Stock Dove** (300 on 28.1.76.), **Woodpigeon** (2,500 on 2.12.73.), **Black-headed Gull** (700) and **Lapwing** (800 on 30.9.73 and 1000 on 18.2.75.). **Golden Plover** were occasional winter visitors, with 4 on 25.3.73. and 12 on 5.12.76.

STAGE 3: 'AREA OF FOSTER'S POND'

To recap, a few fields north of the Watling Street, Bullfurlong Lane petered out into a gated track that led to my pal Peter Rowe's dad's farm. Passing here, and reaching the old Roman highway I would immediately cross into a grassy ride parallel to the road and hedged off on both sides and bordered by a tributary of Soar Brook.

My anticipation, too, would rise here, as towards the end of this strip was a traditional brick-built barn. I don't know its age, but it appears on the 1831 Ordnance Survey map. I have a photograph, in which it looks as though it may have originally been a chapel. During my time this was never in agricultural use and was falling into disrepair; I remember the lath-and-plaster interior walls gradually disintegrating, and there were holes in the tiled roof. But up in the hayloft nested and roosted **Barn Owls**. For my biology A-level dissertation in 1977 I collected and dissected pellets for a whole year. (I warned you about the anorak.) The study was entitled 'Seasonal Variation in the Diet of the Barn Owl' – and a copy of the paper filed in the BTO library. My finding was that, while the owls fed predominantly in winter on field voles (78% of prey weight), in summer their diet was more varied, with close to half (44%) of prey weight made up of wood mouse, bank vole and common shrew, along with the occasional rat, House Sparrow and Starling. Given that the owls could be observed year-round, hunting over the same rough ground and field margins, the conclusion was that it was the prey species rather than the birds that changed their habits in summer, venturing beyond their regular haunts.

BARN OWL
9,000 pairs in 1970s
4,000 pairs in 2020s
55% decline

From my wider ramblings, outwith the scope of this account, **Little Owl** was not uncommon in the general district, but not actually a species I would regularly see on my particular route. The most reliable site was on the very eastern fringe of the area, where Soar Brook cut beneath Lutterworth Road into a damp pasture. This was a popular fishing spot for us as small boys, and we used to guddle for bullhead and stone loach on hot summer days.

During the 1970s **Short-eared Owls** regularly wintered on a large patch of no doubt rodent-rich rough ground beside Stanford Reservoir, 15 miles to the southwest, on the Leicestershire-Northamptonshire border. In January 1979 several took up a roost in stubble fields just north of the Watling Street, and were observed on occasion during the month.

LITTLE OWL
14,000 pairs in 1970s
3,600 pairs in 2020s
74% decline

Moving on from the barn, a stand of willows marked the edge of what, for me, was the best bit of habitat on my entire patch – and as good as any I ever discovered in the wider vicinity.

The public footpath resumed at a crossing point over Soar Brook, this the confluence of two fairly equally sized tributaries. Passing through trees and dense vegetation, the rumble of lorries was left behind, and what seemed to me a kind of wildlife Narnia was entered.

Soar Brook stretched back for a quarter of a mile to its source at Foster's Pond, fringed by an ancient hedgerow that comprised over a dozen species of trees and shrubs, the ditch thickly overgrown in places. To the left was Three-Corner Spinney, and extending from this an area of genuine marsh prolific in plants and invertebrate life. The view ahead was dominated by a line of poplars along the dam of Foster's Pond and a wood behind, its continuation swinging round to the left, this part known as Ash-Pole Spinney. It joined another older copse, Crab-Tree Spinney, from which a high hedgerow ran back to join Three-Corner Spinney and complete the 360-degree amphitheatre.

On 30 June 1974 I conducted a botanical survey of the marsh and Three-Corner Spinney and identified 135 species of plants; a list to which I added roughly another 20 varieties over time. On 28 June 1976 with my friends John Campton and Graham Parker, we ran a generator-powered moth trap on the marsh; we were beset by a blizzard of night-flying insects, and identified 36 species of larger moths.

To stand here early on a still May morning was a magical experience, the air heavy with dew and resonant with birdsong. Against a background beat of the **Cuckoo**, the gentle purr of breeding **Turtle Doves** would emanate from Three-Corner Spinney. A local speciality here was **Garden Warbler**, and typically two males would set up in spring, singing in competition across the marsh, one from willows at the edge of the wood and the other from the thick hedgerow beside Soar Brook.

GARDEN WARBLER
191,000 pairs in 1970s
170,000 pairs in 2020s
11% decline

There would be up to 4 singing male **Reed Buntings** on the marsh, and several pairs of **Starlings** bred in the spinney, which held many old and rotting birches with former woodpecker holes. Not surprisingly, both **Great Spotted** and **Lesser Spotted Woodpeckers** nested here. It was also a regular site for **Willow Tits**. I have notes of a pair excavating a hole 12 feet up the trunk of a birch in Three-Corner Spinney on 11.4.76. and later feeding young on 27.5.76. On another occasion I watched a **Willow Tit** chiselling out a nest hole in a small rotten fence post alongside the brook, and two years later this site was occupied by a pair of **Tree Sparrows**.

WILLOW TIT
57,000 pairs in 1970s
3,400 pairs in 2020s
94% decline

Also here were regular breeding **Whitethroats** (preferring the hedgerow), **Sedge Warbler** (the small willow plantation) and **Willow Warbler** (frequenting willows at the edge of Three-Corner Spinney – as many as 5 singing males in this tight area).

WILLOW WARBLER
4.2 million pairs in 1970s
2.4 million pairs in 2020s
43% decline

Grasshopper Warbler bred in 1975, although it was not an annual visitor. **Skylarks** nested at the dryer margins of the marsh and **Corn Buntings** would sing from the hedgerow that ran from Three-Corner Spinney across to Crab-Tree Spinney.

WHITETHROAT
1.3 million pairs in 1970s
1.1 million pairs in 2020s
13% decline

In winter the marsh, the willows, the overgrown stream and Three-Corner Spinney were frequented by **Common Snipe**, **Jack Snipe**, **Woodcock** and **Water Rail**. I will come back to **Woodcock** shortly, since it was a resident, although I suspect its numbers were supplemented by wintering birds, and sometimes in January up to 3 were disturbed. I only definitely identified **Jack Snipe** on one occasion (1.2.76.) when there was a group of 4 in very cold conditions, although I think there were other unconfirmed sightings. From October through to April, up to 3 **Common Snipe** would regularly rise from the marsh with their signature shriek and zigzag escape flight, while **Woodcock** preferred to feed in the cover of the damp spinney. **Water Rail** could be glimpsed along Soar Brook, scuttling away in the shallows, more likely during the core winter months, November to February, when vegetation was most depleted.

I have one record of a **Green Sandpiper** disturbed from the marsh on 9.12.73. – perhaps a wintering bird. This a species regularly seen on passage at Hinckley sewage farm, 2 miles to the northwest.

Moving on from the marsh, heading alongside Soar Brook towards Foster's Pond, several ivy-covered elms were a regular spot for roosting **Tawny Owls**, and in fact occasional **Barn Owls**, although as an alternative roost to the barn the latter preferred a blasted elm in the hedgerow that cut across the field to Ash-Pole Spinney, which had a great gaping hole halfway up and which served as a nest site in 1976.

Though present throughout the area, right up into the village, **Tawny Owl** was always an exciting and intriguing find for me – perhaps because of my first associations with the bird as a rookie ornithologist, when I discovered that these mysterious night creatures, hitherto only ever heard, could actually be tracked down and observed by day!

Here is an excerpt, quoted verbatim from my very first log book (me aged 11):

February 28th 1971
Woodland Full Of Life

My uncle and I had made our way over the Watling Street and were walking along a footpath towards a tree which we knew was the roosting [sic] of a Tawny Owl, walking was made difficult as the ground was covered in snow which was still falling. When we reached the tree the Owl could not be seen amongst the ivy.

A few minutes later we arrived at the lake known as "Foster's Pond", there were several Coots and Mallards about and the cries of

Moorhens could be heard. A lone Tufted Duck was swimming about and its black tuft was visible through binoculars.

We made our way to the nearby woods and to our surprise we discovered the Tawny Owl sitting in the fork of a tree densely covered in ivy, the bird flew into the trees and we soon heard Jays and Blackbirds mobbing it.

TAWNY OWL
82,000 pairs in 1970s
50,000 pairs in 2020s
39% decline

The hedgerow contained alders and silver birch, and there were more of these catkin-bearers alongside Soar Brook as it headed off on the north side of the Watling Street. Though I rarely recorded **Siskins** on my patch (just a handful of sightings, the most a group of 10 in Three-Corner Spinney), this was always a good place for **Lesser Redpoll**, with regular small numbers year-round, and flocks of up to 20 in winter, for example on 10.11.74. Occasionally I saw **Lesser Redpoll** in my Usual Area, with 5 in a birch in a garden next to my Grandmother's on 25.11.72.

LESSER REDPOLL
1.7 million pairs in 1970s
220,000 pairs in 2020s
87% decline

By way of explanation, my uncle (Bill) referred to above lived with my Grandmother and often accompanied me, with boundless enthusiasm on local walks, and doggedly drove us further afield in his dilapidated Minivan. Up until his sad passing at the age of 93 he loved to hear the accounts of our early expeditions.

I was familiar with this area before I started visiting as a birdwatcher at the age of eleven, and knew the lake as Foster's Pond. On my 1963-surveyed large-scale OS map it is merely described as 'The Lake', as it is to this day. However, on the 1831 OS Map it is called 'Foster's Pond'. It lies within the grounds of a large private house, Leicester Grange, a property that was acquired by John Foster in 1780. The inference is that it dates from this era. It is an artificial water of about 5 acres, formed by a substantial dam that stretches across the shallow 'valley' for some 180 yards. It must have been quite an undertaking in its time.

It was signposted as private property, and contained large carp that I actually caught on occasion by hand as they fed close to the bank – but in all the times I visited I almost never saw a soul, either fishing, or shooting, or walking their dogs, although the grassy banks were generally maintained and kept mowed.

The lake was certainly the iconic feature of the area – in *Middlemarch* open water is to this day a rare commodity. There are no substantial rivers – by definition they start here. Leicestershire's Soar has its source in Warwickshire, in Foster's Pond and ends up, via Nottinghamshire's Trent, emptying into the North Sea as the Humber. For the same reason, there are no reservoirs close by – there simply is not a sufficient watershed, nor the flow to fill and maintain them – and the area lies in the rain shadow of Wales. The main body of water of any note is the Ashby-de-la-Zouch canal, which passes about a mile and a half away, to the west.

In consequence, and perhaps counterintuitively, Foster's Pond was not a magnificent oasis thronged with waterfowl. There simply wasn't enough similar habitat hereabouts to sustain sizeable populations. The regular birds here were limited to **Grey Heron, Moorhen, Coot, Mallard** and – in some years – a pair of **Great Crested Grebes**. The grassy banks also attracted **Pied Wagtail** and **Yellow Wagtail**. **Canada Goose** took up residence in the mid-1970s and grew in number to a peak of 38. The **Grey Herons** nested in the trees on a small island.

GREAT CRESTED GREBE
5,800 pairs in 1990s
4,900 pairs in 2020s
16% decline

Other than **Canada Goose**, in terms of numbers, there were usually just a handful of the abovementioned species, although in winter the **Mallard** flock could reach over 100, and there were odd visits from individuals or small numbers of **Gadwall, Pochard, Mute Swan, Shoveler, Teal** and **Tufted Duck**. **Teal** were the most frequent of these 'vagrants', recorded in all eight of the months between September and April, and once a flock of 50.

LITTLE GREBE
9,700 pairs in 1970s
7,300 pairs in 2020s
25% decline

There are single records of 3 **Little Grebes** on 16.3.75. and a **Cormorant** on 26.12.74.

CORMORANT
10,700 pairs in 1970s
9,000 pairs in 2020s
16% decline

So, Foster's Pond was always interesting at that first glimpse, but generally contained just the handful of residents. The south bank of the pond was bordered by private woodland associated with Leicester Grange. This comprised almost exactly half of a larger wood, divided by a ride along which ran the public footpath. The easterly half is called Ash-Pole Spinney – not an old wood, as the name implies; it is absent on the 1831 OS map but established by the time of the 1886 edition.

The bulk of the land across which I roamed was owned and farmed by Coventry Co-op, and – unlike Foster's Pond and its wood – there was a more relaxed attitude to public access – no signs warning that "Trespassers Will Be

Prosecuted". It no doubt helped that a recognised public footpath passed across the Co-op land.

In this area there was some limited encouragement of **Pheasants**, some rudimentary shooting hides, although no release pens; occasionally I would hear gunfire. I was aware that my dad had shot here on Sunday mornings when I was a very small child; he once brought home a **Pheasant's** egg for me. Pale olive green, rounded and strangely smelling, it is a striking memory that perhaps sparked my early interest in birds.

I would generally follow the public footpath to the top of the ride (in a southerly direction) to check out the fields beyond. There would be small numbers of **Pheasant** and **Grey Partridge**, and in winter **Lapwings** and some gulls. There would be pigeon flocks, including smaller numbers of **Stock Doves**. **Red-legged Partridge** were irregular sightings here, with a pair first seen on 14.5.72. and odd sightings thereafter, generally between March and May, up to 6 birds.

RED-LEGGED PARTRIDGE
150,000 pairs in 1970s
72,500 pairs in 2020s
52% decline

Next, I would veer off from the footpath and plunge into Ash-Pole Spinney. This had been introduced to me as a small boy as 'Bluebell Wood' – and in May it lived up to the epithet, the woodland floor a blurred sea of sapphire and the moist air redolent with the scent of hyacinth. With its origins as a plantation rather than as a semi-natural wood, there was little shrub understory, and it was dry underfoot. The trees were mainly ash, with some English oak and sycamore, and it was certainly less diverse than either of the two older spinneys; Crab-Tree Spinney being more open and dominated by old oaks, and Three-Corner Spinney extremely dense and marshy and characterised by oaks and many birches.

I almost always heard my first **Chiffchaff** of the year in Ash-Pole spinney – usually around 21st March, and certainly before the end of the month – and some years a passing **Wood Warbler** would sing. Indeed in 1977 a male sang continuously from 1st May to at least 4th June, which suggests it attracted a mate. It was also a common haunt of **Blackcaps**, whereas the fringes of Three-Corner Spinney were preferred by their sound-alike cousin the **Garden Warbler**.

WOOD WARBLER
19,000 pairs in 1990s
6,500 pairs in 2020s
66% decline

Ash-Pole Spinney held a good few ivy-covered trees where **Tawny Owl** could be found roosting, and was also the most likely place to see (or at least hear) **Jay** and **Treecreeper** – both elusive species, but present year-round in small numbers. I have maxima for single trips of 6 of each. There were of course the other common woodland species already mentioned, in moderate numbers, but I came across a flock of 80 **Chaffinches** on 30.12.74. **Brambling** was an occasional visitor, here and at other points on my walk, maybe one or two sightings of just a few birds per year – but a larger group of 15 beneath beeches, feeding together with 30 **Chaffinches** on 4.4.76. In my notes I comment upon several striking males of the former.

TREECREEPER
235,000 pairs in 1970s
200,000 pairs in 2020s
15% decline

At the eastern end of Ash-Pole Spinney, another ride separated it from Crab-Tree Spinney – and at this point there were three ponds, linked by a small stream that drained across via a ditch into the marsh – indeed, this 'trickle' was the basis for the existence of the marsh and the boggy nature of Three-Corner Spinney. Two of the ponds were larger than average, and I think owed their origins to the extraction of minerals rather than for livestock watering holes. There was the Black Pit (in the wood itself) and the Green Pit (in the field just beyond). I remember fishing at the Black Pit and catching good-sized roach, despite its unappealing, literally black appearance. The Green Pit was a more pleasing lily-pond, but contained smaller roach and perch. However, these ponds no doubt both held fry, as well as minnows and sticklebacks, and tadpoles, and occasionally I would get a glimpse of a **Kingfisher**. This seemed so incongruous in the rural setting. But with ponds and small lakes dotted throughout the area, and the Ashby-de-la-Zouch Canal as mentioned passing not far to the west, perhaps it should not have been so surprising. There was a further pond, even larger, with a windpump, beyond Crab-Tree Spinney, which I knew as the Mill Pond, although I had also heard it referred to as the Marl Pit, indicating its origins as a source of lime. This, too attracted **Kingfisher**; and I have a particular memory of fishing there on 24.7.74. during a thunderstorm when hundreds of toadlets emerged en masse.

KINGFISHER
7,600 pairs in 1970s
6,400 pairs in 2020s
16% decline

Crab-Tree Spinney was in my estimation an older wood, and this is reflected from the maps, as I have outlined above. The great attraction for me here was in fact a badger's sett, located in a clearing surrounded by old oak and – as is typically the case – overgrown with ancient elders. Foxes also occupied some of the abandoned badger holes. I spent many an evening here watching badgers, and even hosting badger-watching trips in my capacity as Field Officer for Hinckley & District

Natural History Society. I fed badger cubs by hand on grated Red Leicester!

Arriving at dusk to watch the badgers was a wonderfully atmospheric experience. **Barn Owls** would be ghosting over the marsh, and **Tawny Owls** beginning to call. Most remarkable was the roding of **Woodcock** – sitting in silence at the sett its approaching call could be heard, gradually getting louder, an extraordinary triple Snipe-like *thrum* followed by a curious pixie sneeze. In 1976 I heard roding Woodcock as early as 21st March, and that year two birds were observed roding simultaneously on 16th April. They most likely nested in Three-Corner Spinney, which provided both suitable soft feeding ground and extremely dense blackthorn cover which made human disturbance almost impossible.

WOODCOCK
100,000 pairs in 1970s
55,000 pairs in 2020s
45% decline

The more open nature of Crab-Tree spinney some years attracted a singing **Garden Warbler**, and seemed to be preferred by **Willow Warbler** over **Chiffchaff**, the latter more commonly heard in the uniformly wooded Ash-Pole Spinney.

Crab-Tree Spinney was also a regular breeding site for **Spotted Flycatcher**, and the adjacent ponds with hatching insects no doubt contributed to the suitability of this habitat. I recorded 8 individuals, a party of adults feeding young, on 7.9.75.

I saw comparatively few passage migrants in the Area of Foster's Pond – an interesting aspect that my Usual Area was apparently more conducive (the flies from the horse dung, perhaps). I have a couple of individual records of **Wheatear** and **Whinchat** – and one single sighting near Crab-Tree Spinney of a bird I have not yet mentioned, a **Tree Pipit** on 8.9.74.

You might also notice there has been scant reference to birds of prey (owls and Kestrel aside). I have just a handful of records, including **Sparrowhawk** on 20.7.74., **Buzzard** several times between 1.1.73. and 24.12.74. (all in winter), and a single **Merlin** on 18.2.75.

TREE PIPIT
338,000 pairs in 1970s
88,000 pairs in 2020s
74% decline

By now I would be nearing the limit of my walk, ready to turn and head back alongside the hedgerow that connected Crab-Tree Spinney and Three-Corner Spinney, crossing the marsh, Soar Brook and the Watling Street, and past Rowe's farm to pick up Bullfurlong Lane, and thence the footpath to return to my Usual Area.

But there is one final chapter in the quite remarkable story of the Area of Foster's Pond – and that concerns another bird of prey, of sorts ... the **Great Grey Shrike**.

I first saw this species to my heart-bursting excitement at Stanford Reservoir on 14.11.71. It captured my imagination. It was my first local rarity, and found by me, independently.

It was to become a habit.

Two months later I discovered another **Great Grey Shrike** at the Area of Foster's Pond, on 22.1.72. My next was on a field trip to Gibraltar Point on 14.10.73. A bird then reappeared at Foster's Pond on 8.12.74., with further sightings of perhaps the same individual on 22.12.74. and 17.2.75. The same year, but the following winter, there was another at Foster's Pond on 23.11.75.

Incredibly, it seemed, on the first three occasions the bird was in exactly the same place – perched at the eastern side of the triangle of Three-Corner spinney, and visible immediately upon emerging from Crab-Tree Spinney as a distinctive white-grey spot against the dark blackthorn understorey of the copse. I do wonder if this were the same bird, returning to a favourite haunt, despite that it seemed more likely that different individuals were wintering in Britain, moving about the countryside in search of food. Perhaps the vicious blackthorn made a good larder for this notorious 'butcher bird'.

As I grew older and made ornithological connections, and spread my wings as a birdwatcher, I began to come across **Great Grey Shrikes** in Norfolk, with several sightings at Holme Bird Observatory, where it was adopted as the graphic icon of the Norfolk Ornithologists' Association. When I left to go to university in Scotland in 1977 and my new local patch became Fife Ness, I had hardly arrived before I saw my next **Great Grey Shrike** (8.10.77) … and another there on 30.4.78.

After a decade of seeing at least one every year, I took it for granted that this was a species I could expect to see regularly throughout my birdwatching life.

ACTUAL DAYS OUT

The sequence described above is the fantasy day that combines four seasons and all species, something I suppose many of us birdwatchers literally dream about. For a more realistic view, I have copied verbatim two examples of walks from my logbook of 1975, spring and winter.

A SPRING WALK …

Date: 25th May 1975
Location: Usual Route to the Area of Foster's Pond
Time: 07:55 to 10:55
Weather: Broken stratus/altostratus at first, clearing with cumulus building up later; sunny intervals; cool; wind force 1-4 (NE)

Grey Heron 2. Flew from island on Foster's Pond.
Mallard 4.
Canada Goose 8 (4 juv).
Kestrel 1.
Pheasant 2 (pair).
Moorhen 6. Nests on all 3 ponds in the woods.
Coot 2.
Lapwing 20.

Stock Dove 1.
Woodpigeon c.50.
Turtle Dove 1. Heard and seen in Three-Corner Spinney.
Collared Dove 3.
Cuckoo 2. Pair on/around marsh looking for nests. Rufous phase female (although fairly dull).
Swift 2.
Skylark 6.
Swallow 4.
Carrion Crow 6.
Rook 4.
Jackdaw 10. Several nesting in tree holes in woods.
Magpie 4.
Blue Tit 2.
Great Tit 2.
Willow Tit 3. One pair nesting in rotten tree stump on dammed bank of Foster's Pond; hole not naturally formed, but recently excavated. Adults incubating – observed changing places.
Marsh Tit 2.
Wren 8.
Mistle Thrush 8.
Song Thrush c.20.
Blackbird c.50.
Whinchat 1. Male on wire fence of horses' field in Usual Area.
Robin 10.
Blackcap 3. One singing in each of the three spinneys. Often begins with series of churring and grating notes; song

seems more melodious, with more emphasis on each note, whereas Garden Warbler's song is more flowing – notes run together more uniformly.

Garden Warbler 2. One singing at edge of Three-Corner Spinney, the other amongst willows & poplars on dam of Foster's Pond; tends to sing in open more readily than Blackcap; usually longer bursts of song.

Whitethroat 3. Two singing in hedgerows alongside Bullfurlong Lane; other in hedgerow alongside Soar Brook.

Willow Warbler c.10.

Goldcrest 1.

Dunnock c.15.

Pied Wagtail 2.

Yellow Wagtail 2. Feeding on north bank of Foster's Pond.

Starling c.50. Plenty of newly fledged young in family parties.

Greenfinch 2.

Goldfinch 10.

Linnet 2.

Lesser Redpoll 1.

Bullfinch 1 (male).

Chaffinch 4 (males). In song in woods.

Yellowhammer c.10.

Reed Bunting 8.

House Sparrow c.30.

Tree Sparrow 4.

49 species.

AND A WINTER WALK …

Date: 23rd November 1975
Location: Usual Route to the Area of Foster's Pond
Time: 10:45 to 16:00
Weather: Overcast, low stratus layer; dull; cool; had rained overnight; wind force 1-3 (S)

Mallard c.80. On or near Foster's Pond.
Teal 3. As above.
Pochard 1 (male). As above.
Kestrel 2.
Pheasant 7 (6 males).
Water Rail 1. Briefly seen in overgrown ditch of Soar Brook; running about in an attempt to find cover. Lowered head, long beak and striped flanks clearly observed; general plumage grey-brown.
Lapwing c.150. Flock in field N of Watling Street.
Woodcock 1. Flushed from Three-Corner Spinney.
Snipe 1. Flushed from alongside Soar Brook on north side of Watling Street.
Black-headed Gull c.25.
Common Gull c.10.
Herring Gull 2.
Woodpigeon c.100.
Stock Dove c.80. Large flock with some Woodpigeons in field N of Watling Street.
Great Spotted Woodpecker 2 (pair).
Skylark c.10.
Meadow Pipit 6.

Pied Wagtail 6.

Great Grey Shrike 1. First observed at 13:10 perched on small sapling on the marsh, after probably being disturbed from Three-Corner Spinney; seen about an hour later as it flew across the marsh into Three-Corner Spinney.

Wren c.10

Dunnock c.20.

Goldcrest 3.

Robin 4.

Fieldfare c.100. Small flocks in many fields.

Redwing c.100. Some with Fieldfares; flock of 75 near Bullfurlong Lane.

Blackbird c.40.

Song Thrush c.10

Marsh Tit 2.

Willow Tit 2.

Coal Tit 2.

Blue Tit c.30.

Great Tit 4.

Long-tailed Tit c.15.

Yellowhammer 4.

Reed Bunting 4.

Chaffinch c.10.

Greenfinch c.100. Flock in field north of Watling Street.

Goldfinch 3.

Linnet 2.

Lesser Redpoll c.10.

Bullfinch 4.

House Sparrow c.30.

Tree Sparrow c.150. With Greenfinches.
Starling c.30.
Jay 1.
Magpie 2.
Rook 4.
Carrion Crow 4.
Barn Owl – not seen, but 3 fresh pellets in the barn.

Also 49 species.

THE LIST – *MIDDLEMARCH*

Herewith the list of species I recorded on my local patch in the 1970s. The figure in brackets after each bird's name is the maximum I saw on any single occasion, and the description of numbers is an indication of the 'mode' – the regular abundance of that species. So, Starling, for instance – I once recorded 10,000 birds, but more typically on a walk I would see in the range of 20-50 individuals (i.e. present in "good numbers").

KEY
Small numbers = 1-5
Moderate numbers = 5-20
Good numbers = 20-50
Large numbers = 50-100
Very large numbers = 100+

Great Crested Grebe (2) – resident in small numbers
Little Grebe (3) – single sighting 16.3.75.
Cormorant (1) – single sighting 26.12.74.
Grey Heron (5) – resident in small numbers
Mallard (120) – resident in small numbers; winter visitor in large numbers
Teal (50) – occasional winter visitor in mainly small numbers
Gadwall (4) – occasional winter visitor in small numbers

Wigeon (1) – occasional winter visitor in small numbers
Shoveler (1) – single sighting 23.2.76.
Tufted Duck (5) – occasional winter visitor in small numbers
Pochard (2) – occasional winter visitor in small numbers
Canada Goose (38) – resident in small numbers (increasing)
Mute Swan (5) – imm. 28.5.75. and 5 imm. 23.3.76.
Red-legged Partridge (6) – occasional visitor in small numbers, becoming resident
Grey Partridge (30) – resident in moderate numbers
Pheasant (10) – resident in moderate numbers
Buzzard (1) – occasional winter visitor, single birds
Sparrowhawk (1) – occasional visitor, single birds
Merlin (1) – single sighting – 18.2.75.
Kestrel (4) – resident in small numbers
Water Rail (1) – occasional winter visitor, single birds
Moorhen (50) – resident in mainly moderate numbers
Coot (10) – resident in mainly small numbers
Lapwing (1000) – resident in moderate numbers; winter visitor in very large numbers
Golden Plover (12) – occasional winter visitor in small to moderate numbers
Woodcock (3) – resident in small numbers; winter visitor in small numbers
Snipe (4) – winter visitor in small numbers
Jack Snipe (4) – occasional winter visitor in small numbers
Green Sandpiper (1) – single sighting – 9.12.73.
Great Black-backed Gull (5) – winter visitor in small numbers
Lesser Black-backed Gull (60) – winter visitor in mainly small numbers
Black-headed Gull (700) – winter visitor in moderate to large numbers

Herring Gull (50) – winter visitor in small to moderate numbers
Common Gull (10) – winter visitor in mainly small numbers
Stock Dove (300) – resident in small numbers; occasional winter visitor in very large numbers
Woodpigeon (2,500) – resident in large numbers; winter visitor in very large numbers
Turtle Dove (3) – summer visitor in small numbers
Collared Dove (60) – resident in mainly small numbers
Cuckoo (2) – summer visitor in small numbers
Barn Owl (2) – resident in small numbers
Little Owl (1) – resident in small numbers
Tawny Owl (2) – resident in small numbers
Short-eared Owl (6) – winter visitor 22-28.1.79.
Swift (30) – summer visitor in moderate numbers
Kingfisher (1) – resident in small numbers
Great Spotted Woodpecker (6) – resident in small numbers
Lesser Spotted Woodpecker (2) – resident in small numbers
Skylark (53) – resident in moderate numbers; winter visitor in good numbers
Swallow (80) – summer visitor in moderate numbers; passage migrant in large numbers
House Martin (30) – summer visitor in moderate numbers
Wren (15) – resident in moderate numbers
Mistle Thrush (40) – resident in moderate numbers
Fieldfare (200) – winter visitor in good to large numbers
Song Thrush (22) – resident in moderate numbers
Redwing (100) – winter visitor in moderate to good numbers
Blackbird (60) – resident in good numbers
Wheatear (2) – passage migrant in small numbers

Stonechat (2) – winter visitor in small numbers
Whinchat (1) – passage migrant in small numbers
Redstart (1) – passage migrant in small numbers
Black Redstart (1) – single sighting – 29.9.72.
Robin (13) – resident in moderate numbers
Grasshopper Warbler (2) – summer visitor in small numbers
Sedge Warbler (4) – summer visitor in small numbers
Blackcap (6) – summer visitor in small numbers
Garden Warbler (3) – summer visitor in small numbers
Whitethroat (4) – summer visitor in small numbers
Lesser Whitethroat (1) – passage migrant in small numbers
Willow Warbler (15) – summer visitor in moderate numbers
Chiffchaff (4) – summer visitor in small numbers
Wood Warbler (1) – passage migrant and occasional summer visitor
Goldcrest (10) – resident in small numbers
Spotted Flycatcher (8) – summer visitor and passage migrant in small numbers
Pied Flycatcher (1) – single sighting – 11.9.71.
Carrion Crow (11) – resident in small numbers
Rook (250) – resident in large numbers
Jackdaw (60) – resident in moderate numbers
Magpie (10) – resident in moderate numbers
Jay (6) – resident in small numbers
Great Tit (10) – resident in moderate numbers
Blue Tit (30) – resident in moderate numbers
Coal Tit (4) – resident in small numbers
Marsh Tit (6) – resident in small numbers
Willow Tit (8) – resident in small numbers
Long-tailed Tit (15) – resident in moderate numbers
Treecreeper (6) – resident in small numbers

Dunnock (20) – resident in moderate numbers
Meadow Pipit (20) – winter visitor in moderate numbers
Tree Pipit (1) – single sighting – 8.9.74.
Pied Wagtail (70) – resident in small numbers; winter visitor occasionally in large numbers
Grey Wagtail (3) – occasional autumn visitor
Yellow Wagtail (3) – summer visitor in small numbers
Great Grey Shrike (1) – winter visitor, single birds
Starling (10,000) – resident in good numbers; winter visitor in very large numbers
Greenfinch (150) – resident in moderate to large numbers
Goldfinch (46) – resident in moderate to good numbers
Siskin (10) – winter visitor in moderate numbers
Linnet (150) – resident in good to large numbers
Lesser Redpoll (20) – resident in small numbers; winter visitor in moderate numbers
Bullfinch (10) – resident in moderate numbers
Chaffinch (80) – resident in moderate to good numbers
Brambling (15) – winter visitor in small to moderate numbers
Corn Bunting (5) – resident in small numbers
Yellowhammer (60) – resident in moderate to good numbers
Reed Bunting (60) – resident in moderate to good numbers
House Sparrow (850) – resident in very large numbers
Tree Sparrow (150) – resident in moderate to large numbers
Ring-necked Parakeet (1) – single sighting – 19.12.76.

108 SPECIES LATER …

I duplicate below my rating table from earlier:

5 star – "Excellent" – **Cley Marshes**
4 star – "Above average" – **Eye Brook Reservoir**
3 star – "Average" – **Area of Foster's Pond**
2 star – "Below average" – **Usual Area**
1 star – "Poor" – **Fields south of Coventry Road**

Having thoroughly revisited my records for the purposes of writing this account, I am forced to reconsider. Even my humble Usual Area produced many of what, by today's standards, would be classed as 'red-letter' days.

PART II
1974 - 2014
THE NORFOLK YEARS

Outside the Ringing Lab, 1976

THE WREN-PIPIT

Aged 17, in the long, hot summer of 1976 I worked as Honorary Assistant Warden at Holme Bird Observatory (HBO), run by the Norfolk Ornithologists' Association (NOA). A letter from my headmaster had somehow convinced Peter Clarke that he needed the help of a promising biology student. I soon realised that my main duty was to not annoy Peter by asking for things to do. The heat was so oppressive that few people made it up to the observatory; I spent a good deal of time wandering around the vast expanse of deserted dunes and clumps of sea buckthorn, searching for migrants.

On my first day off I drove my battered Fiat to Cley. I noticed the fearsome warden Billy Bishop frowning at my NOA warden's badge; I was charged full price for a permit. I stumbled across the legendary bird artist Richard Richardson lounging on the East Bank in his worn biker's leathers; more generous, he casually pointed out an Aquatic Warbler in a patch of *Suaeda*. However Peter was not as enthused as I might have imagined when I bore this news back to Holme. I deduced there was some internecine rivalry between the ornithological heavyweights of North Norfolk.

Eating my regulation fish supper at Brancaster beach one night I spotted a Mediterranean Gull. Next morning I could tell Peter was not convinced, and I decided I had better refrain from reporting uncorroborated sightings. This dilemma grew wings when I began to get glimpses of a strange bird in the dunes. A demented Wren? A juvenile Meadow Pipit with a stumpy tail? A wren-pipit hybrid? Always in flight, an undulating dot with no field marks – a few squeaks and then it would be gone.

These mystifying glimpses continued, but then the bird disappeared. I was quite relieved, to be frank. Towards the end of my internship, two of my mates – the aforementioned John Campton and Graham Parker – came up from Hinckley for a birdwatching trip. In their mid-twenties they were seasoned spotters. To cut a long story short, late one afternoon we were returning somewhat empty handed from the dunes. The wren-pipit put in a cameo appearance. A conversation ensued:

Me: 'There's that weird wren-pipit thing I've been seeing.'

John: 'That's a Fan-tailed Warbler.'

Me (only previous trip abroad to Isle of Man): 'A what?'

John: 'Fan-tailed Warbler. I've just come back from Fréjus. I've been watching them all week from my balcony.'

Me (pulling the Petersen guide from my rucksack and discovering that against the entry for Fan-tailed Warbler there is not even an 'accidental' triangle for fewer than 20 records): 'It says you don't get them in Britain. It can't be.'

John: '[REDACTED]'

I bolted. The 1976 NOA annual report, authored by Peter Clarke, states: "Hon. Assistant Warden Ian Moore came running to say that a Fan-tailed Warbler had been seen and identified on our car park."

The report rather glosses over the true drama.

Actual conversation:

Me (gasping for breath): 'We've seen a Fan-tailed Warbler.'

Peter (turning away): 'You don't get them in Britain.'

The 'wren-pipit' having spent its time skulking about the vastness of the dunes and who knows elsewhere, by a miraculous piece of serendipity now chose this very moment to perform a fly-past along Broad Water. *Zippity doo dah!* Conversation continues:

Me: *'Peter – there it is!'*

Peter: '[REDACTED]'

For such a mild mannered and quietly spoken man, Peter now revealed a hidden talent for Anglo-Saxon adjectives. (I've often wondered if I'm the only person to have heard him swear.)

Plainly discombobulated, he stomped around a bit. He consulted a few tomes. He wrote some notes. He made a secretive phone call on the rarely used observatory landline. He listened carefully to my friend John's account. And he seemed particularly disquieted when I advanced the theory that the bird might be in residence.

Curiously, his reaction was not the unbridled joy that might have been expected at the appearance of a previously unrecorded species for the UK. On reflection, I understand this. It was Peter's instinct to hide his light under a bushel. It was a trait that he extended to his vocation, with the interests of birds in mind. He didn't really even like ringing, because of its intrusive nature. And visitor income he was happy to keep to a subsistence level. He later told me that he and Jack Reynolds once caught a Thrush Nightingale in the buckthorn near the car park, and they hushed it up to avoid an inundation.

However, I think at some point in the night he must have woken, shouting aloud: *"Cley – put that in your pipe and smoke it!"*

And who could blame him. A British first aside, there were the accounts to think of. So the presence of the 'FTW' (now of course known as Zitting Cisticola) was made public; it remained at Holme for 8 more days, and the relentless influx of twitchers filled NOA's meagre coffers – it was like King's Lynn Town had been drawn against Manchester United in the FA Cup.

For me personally, the experience of 1976 has sustained me down the years – I mean – *Wren-Pipit?* It's not often you get to find *and* name a new species!

NORTH NORFOLK

I hope you can glean from the above account that, by the age of 17, I was already well integrated into the practice of birdwatching in North Norfolk, and moving within its ornithological circles. While researching this book I was honoured to note in the 1976 NOA report under 'Contributors' my name kept auspicious company: the likes of Lord Melchett, R.A. Richardson, P.R. Clarke, G. Parker and J. Campton.

As I have mentioned, I properly started keeping birdwatching logs in 1970, when I was 11 years old. But from the earliest age I had been taken to Norfolk for holidays, for my grandparents had a caravan at East Runton, perched above the sandy cliffs close to Cromer.

As a budding birdwatcher I went on a YOC course based at Sheringham YHA in early April 1974 ... I remember visiting Holme Bird Observatory (quite a trek across the coast) to be greeted by a Long-Eared Owl roosting in a Heligoland trap and my first meeting with the unassuming Peter Clarke. Little did I guess that 2 years later I would be working for him!

And in October 1974 I convinced my parents that half-term in a dilapidated hut on the edge of the salt marsh at Morston would be a good thing. (As an aside, this was the week that Ali miraculously beat Foreman – *The Rumble in the Jungle'* – and my dad, who worked in electronics, drove to Fakenham to borrow a colour TV from a business contact.) Meanwhile I hooked up with a small birdwatching party from Hinckley and I was introduced to Waxwings, Storm Petrel, Little Auk and Rough-legged Buzzard – and I began to realise that Norfolk, like Ali, was in a class of its own. This seemed especially so for a land-locked Midlander largely deprived of water birds and proper heavyweight migration.

In those days there were neither mobile communications nor social media. The Norfolk twitcher's grapevine centred around Nancy's Café in Cley (from which it was almost impossible to move after a helping of her legendary 'Dambuster' bread pudding), where birdwatchers would phone in their sightings and you were expected to answer the phone and write them in the book. I remember the excitement of going there and finding what was about – the beans on toast were my staple lunch.

For some reason, I never became a twitcher – and I was confirmed in the correctness of this decision (for me personally) one time when I was at Holme Bird Observatory. We had netted and ringed a Greenish Warbler. Peter was showing it to a group of birdwatchers whom I did not know. Nor did I suspect they were twitchers until the moment that Peter released the bird. It fluttered towards the belt of pines and the group as one sped off in pursuit, like greyhounds out of a trap, with not a word to us. I was flabbergasted – until I later learnt that to see a bird 'in the hand' somehow didn't count!

Each to their own, and the more people interested in wildlife the better. And, don't get me wrong – a new bird is a genuinely elating experience – but, in mine, ten thousand times more elating when you find that bird yourself. I suppose if I were to compile my own 'British List' it would comprise far fewer species than it might. But no number of 'twitches' or 'assisted ticks' will ever outweigh what I felt for the Fan-tailed Warbler, or my Moulsford Cattle Egret (see the Thames boat illustration later) … or – come to that – my first Goldcrest in my Grandmother's garden, or my first flock of Long-tailed Tits near the Twin Ponds.

There is also the satisfaction of travelling abroad, to discover for oneself what would be British 'rarities' in their native, natural habitats, going about their business, rather than blown off course to Blighty with little hope of anything but extinction. Indeed, to take this a step further, the highlight of my last birdwatching trip to Iceland was not Gyrfalcon, Red-necked Phalarope or Harlequin Duck, but Redwings that I observed feeding young in a wild expanse of willow scrub. To think those nestlings would soon be following my aeroplane … wow.

Moreover, for me, the attraction in nature is in getting to know an area, of studying all forms of its wildlife – not just the birds, but the interdependency of the ecosystem – and of learning its nuances as the seasons go round, year upon year. I might have been a dedicated birdwatcher, but at university I studied both Zoology *and* Botany, and often wondered why they were two separate subjects.

All that said, Norfolk was a place to encounter special birds, and, by visiting often, I was able both to see them and gradually to appreciate the annual ebbs and flows, set against the county's own unique coastal landscape and rainbow skies.

I mentioned above my friends John and Graham, and together with my oldest school pal and fellow adventurer Adrian 'Panner' Bawdon, we formed an ornithological band of brothers. (To this day we have a WhatsApp group name that is not quite printable.) Most significantly, John's family had a caravan at Heacham near Hunstanton.

We made a twice-annual pilgrimage for several days at a time, spring and autumn, and frequent winter day-trips and short breaks in more substantial accommodation with Abbot on tap. And often we took our own family holidays there, and met up.

Between 1975 and 2014 we accumulated 307 days' intensive birdwatching in Norfolk. The anorak not yet abandoned for some trendier garb, I have detailed records of all these visits.

We saw amazing birds. And in the early years we did see many new birds. Our cumulative Norfolk list shot past 250 species in the blink of an eye.

Take the warblers, for instance. By the end of the 1970s we had clocked up Arctic, Aquatic, Barred, Cetti's, Greenish, Fan-tailed, Icterine, Pallas's, Savi's, Yellow-Browed – not to mention the 9 regular British varieties – a remarkable 19 species of warbler (making allowances for the 'FTW'), and these birds that we just happened across, without chasing ticks.

Then there were water birds – gulls, terns, waders, ducks and geese in prodigious numbers – and scarce individual species such as Baird's Sandpiper, Bean Goose, Bittern, Black-necked Grebe, Blue-winged Teal, Broad-billed Sandpiper, Crane, Dotterel, Garganey, Grey Phalarope, Kentish Plover, Long-tailed Skua, Marsh Sandpiper, Pectoral Sandpiper, Red-necked Phalarope, Sabine's Gull, Scaup, Sooty Shearwater, Spoonbill, Spotted Crake, Temminck's Stint and White-rumped Sandpiper.

So, there was always the chance of running into something unusual – certainly this provided a frisson of excitement each time we crossed the county boundary just after Wisbech.

But rarities were fickle.

So, while it is tempting to think of Norfolk as the place for special 'warblers and water birds', for us there was a deeper attachment.

Back lanes and lunch stops

While we mainly plied our trade between the many great sites strung out along the coast, from Snettisham in the southwest to Weybourne in the east, we all agreed – the enduring pleasure of birdwatching in Norfolk was not the enigmatic star of the stage, basking in the uncertain limelight, but the rich background tapestry, enduring and reliable. All those really good places off the beaten track, away from the popular reserves of Cley and (more latterly) Titchwell.

We rarely used the slow coast road to get about – instead we knew long open back lanes that took us at twice the speed and held lesser-known places of interest. We would pause for a lunchtime pint of proper beer at the likes of Stanhoe, Burnham Thorpe or Warham – the Three Horseshoes' garden good for Spotted Flycatcher and Lesser Spotted Woodpecker – and then stop for our snap at a secluded spot where there would be both fuel for the Kelly kettle and birds of no little significance. Sometimes we would linger into the evenings.

There was Salthouse Heath, for instance. In late spring of 1976 we recorded 6 singing male Nightingales and, with great symmetry, 6 Nightjars displaying at dusk. And my notes also mention Red-backed Shrike, Long-eared Owl, 10 Lesser Redpolls, 5 Turtle Doves, 2 Cuckoos, reeling Grasshopper Warbler and the eerie dusk calling of Grey Partridge.

Then there was Ken Hill Wood with its colony of 30 Sand Martins in a tiny abandoned carrstone quarry, swooping about to a musical backdrop provided by 4 more Nightingales. Indeed this record from 15.5.82. includes Green Woodpecker 1, Lesser Whitethroat 1, Garden Warbler 2, Lesser Redpoll 10 and Spotted Flycatcher 1.

There was Ringstead Downs for Lesser Spotted Woodpecker, good old Grey Partridge again, Green Woodpecker, Stock Dove; flocks of Tree Sparrow, Linnet and Yellowhammer; and often migratory Ring Ouzel and Redstart.

There was Brancaster Common for 40 more Sand Martins, Green Woodpecker, 2 Turtle Doves, Cuckoo, 20 Lesser Redpolls (this record 12.5.77.); and always a hatful of resident warblers, for instance 14.5.82. with Whitethroat 10, Blackcap 6, Garden Warbler 2, and a dozen combined Willow-Chiffs.

And there were the back lanes. As we journeyed from place to place, we would catch glimpses of Turtle Dove and Honey Buzzard, and hear snatches of Corn Bunting and Quail. In the evenings we'd be spotting Barn, Tawny and Little Owls as we travelled between our favourite old pubs.

Our local patch in Norfolk

At the heart of this experience – and the reason that Norfolk forms a key part of this narrative – is, once again, the notion of the 'local patch'. Such a place, long watched, tells a story that is not visible in the moment – nor even in the year – and which perhaps only unfolds when the timescale becomes a decade, and longer. And, as you will have gathered from the story of the 'Wren-Pipit', Holme Bird Observatory was our spiritual home in the county – our local patch in Norfolk.

As a brief aside, HBO was founded by Peter Clarke in 1962 and helmed single-handedly through storms of adversity before it eventually achieved the settled status that is apparent today. Without 'PRC' there would be no HBO. He wardened for 33 years, and sadly passed away in 2017, aged 90 – but his spirit still stalks those dunes; I can picture him shambling along the great beach of Holme, those deceptively alert dark eyes one second picking up skuas out to sea, and the next precious amber along the shoreline.

While we ranged all over Norfolk and sometimes into Suffolk, our one consistent move – a kind of ritual – was upon arrival to drop our bags at the caravan at Heacham and make a beeline for the observatory. 'Up Clarkie's' as we called it (and do to this day, as we approach our half-centuries of membership). We had developed a special affinity for the place and a good relationship with its stoic and taciturn warden. Arriving to find Peter, brown as a berry, lounging in front of the old converted pre-war shelter was our means of orientation – to get the lie of the land, and to hear what was about: Peter would actually tell us, and even show us if there was something on the reserve – I recall a magical moment when he lured from the buckthorn a pair of Pallas's Warblers with a secret device! Uncannily, Peter always knew what was about – I think the Fan-tailed Warbler was the only time we surprised him with something.

But – first – we had to arrive.

Turning off the narrow Beach Road from Holme-next-the-Sea and onto the crunch of the shingle-and-sand track always felt like our trip had properly begun.

It is a mile-and-a-half through first rambling gardens and paddocks, with glimpses of the clear-running River Hun, and then between dunes and grazing marshes to the parking area; thence another 300 yards or so on foot amidst buckthorn, brambles and fragrant pines to the original ringing laboratory.

There would be birds on the telegraph wires, on fence posts, on isolated hawthorns; there would be birds in the air – swirling about, passing through – and birds in the bushes (worth at least two in the hand, to a twitcher?).

It could take us an hour to cover the length of the track and the final stretch on foot to the observatory. Someone would shout and we would all jump out. As with all good birdwatching places – we would halt for one thing and find three others. Stop for a Greenland Wheatear and we'd find a Whinchat. And then a Yellow Wagtail. Get back in – "What's that? Stop!" Rinse and repeat. Often there would be semi-rarities like Great Grey Shrike, Hoopoe, Golden Oriole, Wryneck, Richard's Pipit, Tawny Pipit, Water Pipit, Tree Pipit (oh – and *Wren-Pipit)*. In the pines it would be a Redstart and then a Pied Flycatcher – and another – and then a Spotted Flycatcher. If we diverted along the shoreline there could be Twite, Snow Bunting and Shorelark.

Now, there is always the temptation to mention rarities (to which I have succumbed) – but it was the not-so-rarities that made this magic mile what it was – the just-slightly-out-of-the-ordinary chats and flycatchers and pipits – the frequency, the abundance.

You can probably see where I'm headed. And – once again – because I possess copious, comprehensive notes – I have a continuation of the winding narrative which has its roots in my Usual Area. It is a fact, not an opinion.

The fact is the comparison – then, and now. But before approaching the upshot, I need to digress a little.

The Campendium

In 2014, in the 40th year of our Norfolk trips, I had the idea of producing a modest booklet, an almanac that celebrated our birdwatching memories and triumphs.

A regular conversation among our quartet, as we ambled along at Heacham or Holme or Holkham, would begin with the words, *"What year was it we saw the – ?"* (fill in the missing bird's name).

John was most likely to ask this question (and also most likely to be able to supply the answer) – although there was just as often conjecture and disagreement. Knowing I had everything written down, it had never occurred to me to try to remember what year – 1976 was the only one that stuck in my mind – but who could forget a double British first – the Fan-tailed Warbler *and* 76 days of continuous sunshine that no summer since has come close to emulating, regardless of record highs. For us, glowing with sunburn and still basking in the glory of the 'FTW', the season came to a memorable end on 27th August, sheltering beneath the Holkham pines from the mother of all downpours.

The booklet.

To cut to the chase, I went through all my records and produced an alphabetical list of birds (and in some cases notable events of a more infamous nature), and their corresponding dates.

I toyed with various names for this mini-publication – not least, Old Moore's Anorak – but I erred towards the 'Compendium' – which then naturally evolved into the 'Campendium' in honour of John (Campton), as our Rememberer-in-Chief.

This earlier act of interrogating my Norfolk records was not unlike the job I have since done for my local patch in *Middlemarch* for the purposes of this book. Indeed it was something of a precursor, as a practical challenge (many, many hours of detailed work). The similarity did not end there.

I had forgotten how many birds there used to be.

Or perhaps there was another way of looking at this.

We had not noticed how few birds there were now.

Okay, I think we harboured a sense of decline, without actually putting it into words – and I suspect that subliminally it wasn't something we wished to recognise. But we always kept a list for the trip and what was apparent was that it became progressively harder to reach the magic number 100 – I think we put it down in part to us just getting old and lazy. Occasionally we would notice something was missing. But there were also trips when you couldn't buy a Song Thrush, or couldn't turn your head and not see a Jay – chance migration events or short-term population wrinkles that ironed themselves out. But the century seemed increasingly elusive. When I produced the Campendium I did a quick calculation. Our trip lists in the 1970s reached as high as 115 species – by now we were toiling to reach 90.

Facing up to it, the Nightingales had disappeared from Salthouse Heath and Ken Hill Wood (along with Nightjars at the former); there were no longer Corn Buntings strung along the wires above the back lanes; Willow Tit and Marsh Tit had just fallen off a cliff, and Tree Sparrow, Turtle Dove and Lesser Spotted Woodpecker had not featured for years.

But what stood out most of all – and I have alluded to this above – was how many interesting birds (and how *many* of them) we used to see at Clarkie's. As I have described, in the 1970s and early 1980s it seemed like we had to fight our way through the sightings to reach the observatory. Now we were sailing by, largely undistracted.

Here is a representative comparison, taken from my records.

SPRING VISITS TO HOLME BIRD OBSERVATORY, HIGHLIGHTS:

6 MAY 1976	10 MAY 2013
Marsh Harrier 2	Whimbrel 1
Short-eared Owl 1	Marsh Harrier 1
Grasshopper Warbler 1	Lesser Whitethroat 1
Pied Flycatcher 2	Cuckoo 1
Redstart 1	
Whinchat 10	
Wheatear 20	
Ring Ouzel 1	
Tree Sparrow 50	
Turtle Dove 3	
Yellow Wagtail 1	
Redpoll 10	

At the risk of tedium I would include more of these tables – but, as I discovered when I compiled the Campendium, *recent* records were few and far between. Despite our best efforts we simply weren't seeing birds on the way up to the observatory that would break through as literally noteworthy highlights.

Now, of course, I should acknowledge that there is a far more comprehensive HBO record – begun in 1962 by Peter Clarke – but on the face of it, it reflects our trend. For example, at the time of writing I have just received the 2021 NOA annual report. Take August of that year. I have shown below the combined best day total for the *entire month* (i.e. the peak daily counts, not necessarily seen together). I have compared it to a *single day* in August from Peter's 1976 report, the 22nd of the month.

NOA REPORTS FOR HOLME BIRD OBSERVATORY, 1976 v 2021:

AUGUST 1976 **Single day, 22nd**	AUGUST 2021 Peak daily count
Willow Warbler 40	Willow Warbler 3
Garden Warbler 6	Garden Warbler 1
Whitethroat 6	Whitethroat 8
Lesser Whitethroat 6	Lesser Whitethroat 2
Spotted Flycatcher 2	Spotted Flycatcher 1
Pied Flycatcher 24	Pied Flycatcher 3
Whinchat 6	Whinchat 0
Wheatear 24	Wheatear 2
Redstart 4	Redstart 1

Peter also recorded a Tree Pipit and a Wryneck on 22nd August 1976. (The Spotted Flycatchers were in fact the following day; I include these for symmetry.)

I would not be surprised if the overall species counts for 1976 and 2021 were on a par, perhaps even higher for the latter as there are so many more birdwatchers nowadays and few feathered visitors escape scrutiny. But today's absolute numbers cannot hold a candle to those of yesteryear.

Four calling birds

The first trip upon my compiling of the Campendium was 2014. Despite that the list reminded us of all the great birds our quartet had found in Norfolk, and was cause for celebration of the Greene King variety, I think we all had a sense that the best days were behind us. For myself, in particular – alone in having delved through our records – it was not so much that so many rarities were in our rear-view mirror, but the dramatic dearth of formerly common interesting birds.

I can't say there was a single moment of epiphany that prompted me to author this entreaty on behalf of our *Lost Birds* – but I do recall a small juxtaposition of events that precipitated a change in awareness.

On that trip we were struggling for birds – we knew

that. You can only spend so much time at the nature reserves, and for birdwatchers who want to find their own sightings, away from the telescope-toting hordes, these places have limited appeal in any event. There was made the suggestion that we try Courtyard Farm near Ringstead, the environmentalist Lord Peter Melchett's land. He was well known and lauded for his conservation-minded approach, and there were good reports in years past of plenty of birdlife.

But this particular afternoon we spent two hours finding 4 Mistle Thrushes.

And then came the stark comparison.

The next day, I returned home to Edinburgh and counted 40 species of birds on a walk from my front door. I live on Corstorphine Hill, adjacent to the eponymous local nature reserve.

Now, as it happens, Corstorphine Hill will form part three of this mini-trilogy – and will not deviate from the underlying narrative. But on this particular day – the day after the 4 Mistle Thrushes – the contrast was stark.

Norfolk – if I may share one of the gang's ornithological euphemisms – was ducked.

This was not something I was happy about or even willing to acknowledge, but it seemed to me that 307 days' intensive birdwatching spanning 5 decades of observation could not lie.

PART III
2006 - PRESENT
CORSTORPHINE HILL

Clinging on ... until 2017

DÉJÀ VU?

These days, Corstorphine Hill LNR in Edinburgh is my local patch. LNR stands for local nature reserve, and it is a genuinely wild habitat within the city limits. I am a member of the committee that oversees the reserve and have the honorary role of Wildlife Liaison Officer – dealing on the one hand with the City of Edinburgh Council, and on the other communicating with the wider community. As part of our public information programme and service to members I conduct guided bird and wildflower walks, and give talks from time to time. I also produce a photographic blog *Chilloutdoors* which follows the wildlife of the hill as the seasons go round. This can be found at https://chilloutdoors.tumblr.com.

I recently wrote a wildlife summary for our website – *A Quick Tour of the Biodiversity of Corstorphine Hill* – and I include here some of this account, which both sets the scene for the next act of this avian chronicle and mirrors the emerging thesis.

Bird factory

In 2006 I began systematically recording the wildlife of Corstorphine Hill, visiting on an almost daily basis. I was immediately struck by the abundant bird life. As a rule of thumb, I judged there to be about *twice* as many species, and *four times* as many birds compared to 'typical' countryside. As recently as 2016, 46 species bred on or in close association with the hill, comprising an estimated 750 pairs. Migratory, wintering and passing local birds have lifted my cumulative list to 108 species (an uncanny symmetry with *Middlemarch*, also 108). All in all, not bad for a site barely two miles as the crow flies from Princes Street and within a metropolitan area inhabited by almost a million people.

If I include the Water of Leith, which marks the foot of the hill at Roseburn and the line of the long-drained Corstorphine Loch, I can add Dipper, Goosander, Grey Heron, Grey Wagtail, Kingfisher, Mallard, Moorhen and Mute Swan to the breeding list.

From my attic on the hill as I have written this book I have experienced eye-level close encounters with Buzzard, Kestrel, Merlin, Osprey, Peregrine, Red Kite, Sparrowhawk and Tawny Owl. Right now, a family of four Pentland Hills Ravens cavorts on the wind, buzzed by a squadron of local Jackdaws.

So, why so many birds?

The watchpoint aspect of the hill aside, a simple answer can be deduced by looking at what we do to make our gardens bird-friendly. We put out food and we hang nest boxes. Something to eat, somewhere to breed; this is all birds ask of their environment, and they are remarkably tolerant of human intrusion.

An experiment in 2021, in which the reserve's boundary hedgerow alongside Clermiston Road was allowed to grow from its normally severely cut 'fencing' style, saw 43 birds' nests built in a half-mile stretch. From zero to 43 in one summer! The species were Blackbird, Bullfinch, Dunnock, Greenfinch, Song Thrush and even Woodpigeon. Once vacated, many of these nests were then repurposed by fieldmice to store rose hips for the winter. No, the wildlife does not ask for much.

Floribunda

I began to survey the flora of the hill. I was astounded to find 43 species of trees and 26 species of shrubs. To date, I have identified 136 species of flowering herbs, having added 10 grasses in the past year.

There are exotic-sounding specimens like perforate St John's wort, hemp agrimony and climbing corydalis, and the list incorporates a remarkable 19 species that are recognised as 'marker plants' for ancient woodland, such as wood anemone, pignut and dog violet.

People who know better than me have identified 26 liverworts and 82 mosses; more modestly, 4 species of ferns are readily visible to my less-trained eye.

A vast array of fungi can be found throughout the year (but particularly in autumn), and these include some of the more distinctive species like artist's fungus, black bulgar, common stinkhorn, death cap, earth star, fly agaric, jelly ear, lawyer's wig, parasol mushroom and razor strop.

So here is part of the answer.

There is an unprecedented diversity of flora (taking a liberty with the classification of fungi), and this is at the root of a plentiful and varied food supply. Not only in spring and summer when birds are breeding, but also in winter. Redwings come for the berries of holly and whitebeam, Crossbills for the seeds of Scots pine and Norway spruce, Siskins for larch, and Redpolls for alder and birch. During 'mast years' hundreds of Woodpigeons gorge upon the nuts of beech, along with small numbers of Bramblings.

Invertebrates

The wealth of flora is also the basis for a copious population of invertebrates, most obviously insects and spiders. Many birds are at least part-carnivorous, and this is particularly evident in spring when gangs of adult Starlings descend to load their beaks with hatching St Mark's flies, and in early autumn when passage migrants such as Spotted Flycatchers, Swifts and House Martins stop off to feed on airborne insects.

A remarkable 53 species of hoverflies have been identified on the hill; there are 10 regular species of bumblebees, and a yet-to-be counted number of wasps – although 3 species are known to nest in the stock of a single rotting beech tree.

The invertebrate population sustains many resident bird species, from Goldcrests to Jackdaws to Great Spotted Woodpeckers, along with Swallows and 4 regular species of warblers that come from Africa to breed: Blackcap, Chiffchaff, Whitethroat and Willow Warbler.

Holes, height & hideaways

The second key plank in explaining the avian abundance is found in the trees and shrubs – and this is from the perspective of nesting rather than food. 13 of the bird species that breed on the hill are hole-nesters. These range from Treecreeper to Stock Dove, and from Great Tit to Tawny Owl. For holes, it is necessary to have *old* trees. They lose branches and they grow cracks, folds and crevices. Using a method called Mitchell's Rule it is possible to age a tree from its circumference; some of the larger oaks and beeches may be three hundred years old (noting that 'Beechwood House' on the south side was built in 1780). In 2021, a single ancient beech tree was home to Blue Tit, Great Spotted Woodpecker, Jackdaw, Kestrel, Mistle Thrush, Nuthatch, Stock Dove and Woodpigeon – a nature reserve in its own right! Large, tall trees are also essential to provide nesting sites high in the canopy for birds such as Buzzard, Carrion Crow, Mistle Thrush and Sparrowhawk.

Surprisingly, it is a sycamore which takes the prize for the greatest girth – a giant specimen of almost 18 feet; going by Mitchell's rule it could date from the time of the Great Plague, and though a much-maligned species, and not a great 'nesting tree', the sycamores on the hill feed St Mark's flies with their nectar, and supply the likes of Blue Tits and especially Treecreepers with a year-round diet of sycamore aphids, in their various life-cycle stages; some 40 billion available, at the best estimate.

The key matter of suitable breeding sites extends to the shrubs and undergrowth, most notably the extensive patches of gorse, brambles and willowherb. This dense, almost impenetrable habitat provides protected nesting for as many as 16 species of birds, such as Dunnock,

Greenfinch, Song Thrush and the comparatively scarce Whitethroat, as well as hosting a locally important population of Long-tailed Tits.

Animal soup

The exceptional biodiversity of the hill is reflected in other classes of animals, such as – to take a couple of the more conspicuous examples – butterflies and mammals.

17 species of butterflies have been recorded, and there are indigenous populations of comma, green-veined white, meadow brown, orange tip, ringlet, small copper and speckled wood (and more recently small skipper), along with day-flying cinnabar and silver Y moths. Other moth species identified include ghost swift, light emerald, peppered moth and poplar hawk.

For a suburban site there is a remarkable mammal population, of about 15 species. This includes badger, common shrew, fox, long-tailed fieldmouse, Natterer's bat, pipistrelle bat, rabbit, roe deer and short-tailed vole. Despite the lack of year-round standing water, amphibians are represented by common frog and common toad, and actually manage to breed in damp spring seasons, at times using the ancient wells. Palmate newts inhabit garden ponds on the hill, including my own.

Accident of history

If the 'first level' answer to the question, 'Why the great diversity of birds?' is the diversity of plants, fungi and invertebrates, the 'second level' question is 'Why the diversity of plants, fungi and invertebrates?'

A clue to this can be found by comparison with the golf courses that border the nature reserve on its north-eastern flank. Nice and green-looking (no pun intended), and a far preferable buffer than a housing estate, *but pretty much a monoculture*. Rarely are there any birdies on the fairways, whereas the patches of rabbit-grazed grassland on the reserve – or indeed the tussocky zebra enclosure of Edinburgh zoo – are frequented by voraciously feeding Stock Doves, Jackdaws, Starlings and thrushes.

Since Stone Age peoples carved their mysterious cup marks in the ice-scarred dolerite on Corstorphine Hill some 5,000 years ago, it has been an almost exclusively organic environment.

That said, the hill's wildlife has been greatly influenced by human hand. Old maps and traditional lore suggest it was predominantly farmed for sheep before the advent of the main woodland in the 19th Century, and was certainly hunted over from the various estates (Beechwood, Clerwood, Craigcrook, Hillwood and Ravelston) which shared its territory. Many of the tree species are likely to have been introduced as part of a Victorian fashion for the arboretum, and more recently shrubs have escaped from adjacent gardens, not always to good effect.

Creeping threats

Indeed, encroachment by invasive species is a real and present danger to the more indigenous wildlife. Salmonberry in particular is aggressively crowding out the 'native' flora, and could eventually blanket the entire hill, preventing even tree regeneration. Himalayan and yellow balsam represent a lesser but not insignificant threat. Meanwhile, the precious gorse which supports many classes of wildlife is highly susceptible to damage from fires, started both carelessly and in some cases maliciously.

A second issue of concern is the relentless residential development taking place in Edinburgh. The capital's population is growing at almost 8% per annum, a product of net migration. As old houses, hotels and hospitals are converted into apartments, student flats and care homes, large areas of rambling gardens are lost to parking spaces, degrading the natural value of the 'apron' or green buffer zones and wildlife corridors that help sustain wildlife populations on the reserve itself.

Sounds familiar

This is where I come to *déjà vu*, the title of this section.

As I have suggested, almost a decade before I got around to interrogating my records for this book, the seed was planted in my mind by the stark contrast of one day scratching about for 4 Mistle Thrushes in Norfolk, and the next – and here's the irony – the teeming birdlife of Corstorphine Hill.

Irony, because little did I suspect that the straws blowing innocuously in the bracing Scottish breeze would coalesce and in time clonk me on the back of the head like a whacking great bale falling off the back of Peter Rowe's dad's haycart. I was about to bear witness to another cycle of decline.

On reflection, I had already noticed that Yellowhammer had been absent from the hill, but in a small way its disappearance was offset by the arrival in January 2011 of Nuthatch, a larger-than-life species that began to entertain the locals.

But this uptick proved to be a chimera.

To step aside for a moment from straight statistics, and make a more qualitative assessment, at the time of writing my status report would be along these lines:

GOING (WELL) ...

The indigenous birds that require comparatively small territories continue to thrive, since their populations are self-replicating. These would include the resident thrushes and tits, finches and crows, gulls and pigeons; Blackcap and Chiffchaff; Great Spotted Woodpecker and Nuthatch; Dunnock, Wren and Robin; and Starling and House Sparrow (the latter for which I have a mini breeding programme, a small colony in my garden, with year-round seed and a terrace of nest boxes).

Also holding up are regularly visiting Ravens; good numbers of southbound Spotted Flycatchers in August (yes, Spotted Flycatchers are doing fine, somewhere across the North Sea); and the seasonal flypasts of Pink-footed Geese and Ospreys, which use the hill as a navigational beacon. Down on the Water of Leith, Goosander in winter often number up to 30 and now breed in the city. Likewise, Dipper, Mallard and Moorhen could be added in this regard.

In total, the 'Going Well' list comprises some 35 species.

GOING (DOWN) ...

The birds of the hill that I worry about are, first of all, those with just a handful or fewer breeding pairs. These include all four birds of prey (Kestrel having flirted with a tentative return in the past two years), Jay, Long-tailed Tit, Treecreeper, Mistle Thrush, Whitethroat, Willow Warbler and Goldcrest.

Secondly, those more peripheral species that come to feed, House Martin, Swallow and Swift, along with Grey Wagtail and Grey Heron are all now scarce and in long-term decline, as are numbers of passage migrants such as Meadow Pipit, Redstart, Skylark and Wheatear. Wintering Redwings are reducing year on year, Fieldfares are now a rarity, and sightings of Crossbill, Redpoll, Siskin and Woodcock about half as frequent as in 2014.

The 'Going' list comprises 24 species. With several just clinging on, it would not take much to lose any or all of these, as witnessed by the next category.

GONE ...

In the last decade, the following breeding species have all but disappeared from the hill:

1. Yellowhammer
2. Collared Dove

3. Green Woodpecker
4. Kestrel
5. Linnet
6. Pheasant
7. Pied Wagtail
8. Rook

To add insult to injury, through my involvement with Edinburgh Natural History Society I was presented with historical records made on Corstorphine Hill, dating from the 1970s. The breeding losses mount:

9. Hawfinch
10. Spotted Flycatcher
11. Tree Sparrow
12. Wood Warbler

There's our Spotted Flycatcher again – as mentioned above, nowadays exclusively an autumn passage migrant. Tree Sparrow – I have recorded only a single bird on the hill (exactly the same number of sightings as I have had of Alpine Swift). Wood Warbler – 2 singing males, briefly in spring – although I know of a breeding site not far away in West Lothian. Hawfinch, hmm.

So – there *were* 50 breeding species – 12 have gone, that's almost a quarter since the 1970s and 16% of those present just a decade ago.

With this in mind, I checked the average monthly totals from my records for Corstorphine Hill. These are not necessarily breeding birds, but all species noted, including those passing.

2014: average 47 species recorded per month
2021: average 39 species recorded per month

… and hence my use of the expression *déjà vu*.

EPILOGUE

Field elms

TRIUMPH OR ILLUSION?

Viewers of TV documentaries could be excused for thinking everything in the wildlife garden is rosy. There is an extraordinary fruitfulness to be enjoyed, and skilled photography and subtle anthropomorphism makes these programmes compelling viewing.

Visit an RSPB reserve and you will likely find it teeming with birds – great flocks of waders or wildfowl, a cacophony of warblers, majestic raptors – and maybe even a Tree Sparrow or two.

And there are those birds brought back from the brink, the likes of Avocet, Bittern, Black-tailed Godwit, Chough, Cirl Bunting, Corncrake, Dartford Warbler, Osprey and Stone Curlew. Many of these are RSPB success stories, conservation triumphs of the past half-century; and there have been audacious reintroductions like Crane, Great Bustard, Red Kite and Sea Eagle.

Not all species have declined. Buzzard and Sparrowhawk would now be regulars at the Area of Foster's Pond, when before they were occasional visitors, and Peregrine not an uncommon sight in the vicinity. Raptors like these have benefited from changes in agricultural practice, most notably the ban on DDT in 1986. There are species that have expanded under their own steam – Cetti's Warbler; Little Egret and its allies; Nuthatch has marched all the way from Leicestershire when I was a boy to my garden feeder in Edinburgh.

Blackcap, Carrion Crow, Chiffchaff, Goldfinch, Great Spotted Woodpecker, Great Tit, Jackdaw, Long-tailed Tit, Magpie, Mallard, Stock Dove and Woodpigeon have all as good as doubled or better since the 1970s.

Part of the Union

Politically, the 1970s was a tumultuous era, ushered in by a surprise victory for Ted Heath over Harold Wilson; characterised by more days lost to strikes than any other decade since the 1920s; and marched out by the scruff of its neck at the hands of workaholic Margaret Thatcher. And there was the musical backdrop of *'Part of the Union'*, the signature anthem for the times, by the rock band *Strawbs*, which peaked at No.2 in February 1973.

But it was another kind of union for which 1973 will be remembered, for Britain joined the EEC. The Common Agricultural Policy came into effect.

Sacré bleu!

For pretty much all of recorded history, farmers were obliged to grow what they could sell. Now they were able to *sell what they could grow*. This sounds like a sematic trick – but for the countryside the distinction was profound.

Throughout Europe, and indeed the world, changes in farming practices have coincided with a catastrophic collapse in bird populations. The RSPB estimates that

Britain has lost over 40 million birds since 1966, and that together with the European Union we have lost a net 600 million birds since 1980. If you add up just the species I have included in this book – based upon government and RSPB statistics – the UK figure looks like a serious understatement as far as the threatened species are concerned. France has lost one third of its birds in the past 15 years. In North America the figure is estimated at a jaw-dropping 3 billion.

I have seen the endless wheatfields of the American Midwest. I have seen the palm oil plantations of Borneo that mock the receding rainforest. I have seen the green fertiliser-fed waters of Halong Bay.

Closer to home, I saw Dutch elm disease arrive in the late 1960s. Innocuous at first, by 1980 it had killed 20 million field elms, predominantly in southern Britain. Decimate was not the word, despite its demotic allure. In the headlong rush to maximise acreage and yield, the loss of our elms made the grubbing-up of hedgerows far less problematic. Meanwhile, the agrochemicals industry was entering a boom that would continue to this day. In 2021 its market size was equivalent to the annual worldwide revenues of McDonald's.

I recall my youngest daughter asking me why there was a road through a cornfield in East Lothian (she pointed out the tracks made by a big-boom sprayer).

Sadly, she is more observant than most, and these changes have passed largely unnoticed. To the untrained eye, the broad-brush sweep of the British countryside looks much the same, with or without its wildlife.

When I left *Middlemarch* for St Andrews University in 1977, my parents moved to London. I had limited cause to go back to the Midlands. But I did revisit the Area of Foster's Pond on one occasion, these notes – albeit brief and incomplete – sound something of a death knell.

30 August 1978

Elms dying everywhere – small-leaved elms in Ash-Pole Spinney, English elms and hedge gone in main field (Barn Owl) & wych elms by Soar Brook (Tawny Owl). Barn demolished (Barn Owl, Stock Dove). Marsh drained.

A quick glance at Google Maps reveals my old haunts either to have disappeared under brick and tarmac or changed beyond recognition. Great swathes are given over to warehousing, hotels, a motorway. Now streets and driveways and houses and industrial units sit where once Yellow Wagtails were chased by Cuckoos; where flocks of Tree Sparrows and Linnets swirled above the corn; where Grasshopper Warblers and Corn Buntings sang their melancholy refrains, lamenting what was to come.

When I look back and reflect upon my local patch in those days, I see there was a matrix of smallish fields bordered by high, dense hedgerows and herb margins, a scattering of ponds, of low-intensity agriculture, and of small but productive oases such as my Usual Area with its rambling orchards and paddocks, and the Area of Foster's Pond, with its marsh, woods and watercourses.

I thought it was boring farmland, uninspiring – worth only between 1 and 3 stars on my scale – *but it was rich farmland.*

In conversation with my friends in the know, we estimate that of the 60 species formerly in my Usual Area only 20 species would now occur.

This can be viewed as a simple matter of displacement, but of equal concern are those *Lost Birds* that are no longer found in what countryside remains.

You will have spotted the 'shrinking birds' that illustrate the statistics, the stark numbers that – even if only roughly accurate – chart the decline of the birds of this depleted environment. We reckon a typical full walk today would find only *half* the species of those actual visits I documented in May and November of 1975. And of the remaining half, many would be fewer in number. A flying visit to the Area of Foster's Pond in March 2023 produced only 17 species.

I would love to be proved wrong – if someone can tell me that Lesser Spotted Woodpecker, Garden Warbler, Turtle Dove, Willow Tit and Woodcock all still breed in Three-Corner Spinney I would be cock-a-hoop! But more chance, methinks, of finding the Loch Ness monster. Instead I have to settle for them in my mind's eye, their spirits living on in my old notes and logbooks.

The statistics for North Norfolk tell a similar tale – the comparison that a day in 1976 produced more birds than a month in 2021 is mind-boggling. Yet, while *Middlemarch* has changed almost beyond recognition, North Norfolk has seen little development, and looks much the same now as it did back in the 1970s. Indeed, there are more reserves and wiser, better-funded conservation efforts. And while *Middlemarch* birds were predominantly sedentary in British terms, Norfolk birds comprise a much more significant visiting constituency. That fewer visit each year points to a wider explanation.

Clearly, population is just one factor in the equation. Certainly, in my lifetime the population of England has increased by 15 million people. Demand on land does not require a rocket scientist to predict the outcome for one of the most densely populated countries on the planet.

But in the same period the population of Scotland has remained static, resolute at just 5 million for the last half-century. A country two-thirds the area of England, with one-seventh of the population density, yet the decline of Britain's birds has not stopped at Hadrian's Wall. Sixteen years and some 5,000 daily walks on Corstorphine Hill are testament to that.

It's not just the land, it's the use.

What I described in my log book on 30th August 1978 was the pincer movement of Dutch elm disease and the Common Agricultural Policy. These changes must already have been taking place, but perhaps the hiatus in my long-established routine enabled the scales to fall from my eyes.

When I go out every day I still think Corstorphine Hill is a wonderful place, brimming with birds and many other classes of wildlife. In April the birdsong in the woods is of orchestral proportions, and before daybreak in May the hill floats on a dawn chorus of Blackbirds that rises up from the surrounding suburbs like the morning mist. My weekly blog demonstrates just how good the place is. BBC's *Winterwatch* even came here in 2023!

But when the longer view is taken, it becomes difficult not to mention the casualties, and those in jeopardy. I am always torn as to whether I should include this chronic aspect in my talks and guided walks. It feels like tempting fate, but there is no escaping the fact that Corstorphine Hill has lost a quarter of its breeding birds since the 1970s.

These are not exactly rare birds, but locally semi-scarce species that simply do not have the numbers in the surrounding countryside to repopulate losses from natural attrition. When the female Green Woodpecker of the pair that thrived on the yellow meadow ants of the southern slope was killed by a Sparrowhawk in January 2017, the male called for a mate for almost 7 weeks. On 21st March, the first day of spring, he gave up. He left.

It is ironic, when the perfect habitat is ready and waiting – but a salutary reminder that 'island' reserves can last only so long – like Noah's Ark they offer a limited window of survival for the species they harbour. The biological clock was ticking, and there was no surfeit of Green Woodpeckers to be drawn from the surrounding countryside.

I have spoken of two of the pressures that threaten Corstorphine Hill, invasive strangulation and urban encroachment – but the elephant in the room is further afield. Literally, afield. If you consider the list of *Lost Birds*, the majority are species of rich farmland. Perhaps with a couple of exceptions, most are just the kind of birds I was accustomed to seeing in 1970s *Middlemarch* and Norfolk.

Corstorphine Hill, with its varied habitats offers exactly this mixture of grassland, scrub and woodland fringe, and – were it ten or twenty times the area – it might just support self-sustaining populations of rich farmland birds (in the way that it does foster its indigenous woodland birds).

That until recently so many species hung on is something of a small miracle – and testament to a biodiversity borne out of freedom from agrochemicals and the scourge of land management designed to maximise crop yield.

The recovery of ELMS?

A somewhat ironic acronym, 'ELMS' stands for Environmental Land Management Schemes. The UK government's website is more specific, listing 3 schemes: the Sustainable Farming Incentive, Countryside Stewardship and Landscape Recovery'. ELMS are intended to reward environmental land management – more prosaically, "public money for public goods". ELMS apply to England only; the devolved administrations of Northern Ireland, Scotland and Wales are developing their own policies for agriculture and the rural environment.

Is this a light at the end of the tunnel – or just a combine harvester coming the other way?

I have spent the majority of my working life running my own businesses, so I am no stranger to the concept that, without a profit being made there is no business – no investment, no jobs, no tax revenue, no public services. And the status quo is an unachievable concept; the turnover graph must go up; else it goes down. Growth is the only strategy that is viable for an enterprise in the long term. And the microeconomics of the firm are the macroeconomics of the economy; a growing population, 8 billion and counting, demands an ever-growing GDP. And pizza.

That the launch of ELMS has been buffeted by forces of war, pestilence and famine is a reminder that this is a worldwide issue. But in the first instance it offers for the UK a ray of hope. And in our world-leading conservation organisations like the RSPB we have the knowhow, the commitment and the reserves – the 'arks' – from which to repopulate our restored countryside.

Making birds count

But 'war, pestilence and famine' is not some literary device. These features form part of the practical compromise that has to be recognised. Humanity is faced with existential choices – including what kind of existence it wants.

Umbilically connected is the further question of the moral obligation of humans to the planet, and to the moral rights of wildlife; for their part, our fellow time travellers do not have much of a voice.

Whatever one's position on the great spectrum of belief, there is a simple fact on which most people would agree: that the world in which we find ourselves is a better place for its biodiversity.

The hedgerow that borders the west side of Corstorphine Hill is a better place for one small decision, to retire the chainsaw. The corollary: from zero to 43 nests in a single season. There are spring blossoms and autumn berries. There is winter succour for fieldmice. If you are waiting for the 26 bus it is more pleasing on the eye and its denizens melodic to the ear.

And what of those car windscreens?

Perhaps one day soon there *will* be a splat-free car, the green automobile that diverts winged insects safely over the vehicle. Perhaps low-flying creatures – just like the pale phenotype peppered moth, post-Industrial Revolution – will stage an evolutionary comeback.

And perhaps, just perhaps – riding the slipstream of so much to eat – there really will be an explosion in the population of the Spotted Flycatcher.

They will nest again on Corstorphine Hill, Salthouse Heath, Ken Hill Wood, Crab-Tree Spinney … and perhaps even the countryside of *Middlemarch*, newly rewilded in many small but significant ways, where a child will venture out, binoculars poised, pen and notebook at the ready … and discover not *lost*, but *lots* of birds to count.

APPENDICES

Making birds count

THE DATA

The data for the repetitive statistics which chart the decline of *Lost Birds* arise from two primary sources. Firstly, the percentage change figure is taken from a UK Government report, *Wild Bird Populations in the UK, 1970 to 2019*, which can be found at the first link below (apologies for the inconvenience if you are reading a printed version of this book). For the majority of bird species this relates to the period from 1970, although in some cases the measurement interval begins more recently, and this is stated accordingly.

Secondly, the current population figure, number of pairs, is taken from the RSPB website.

These two factors are then combined to extrapolate the 1970s population figure. For example, Tawny Owl has declined by 39% and there are 50,000 pairs. Thus, there were approximately 82,000 pairs of Tawny Owls.

In case you hadn't noticed, the idea of the smaller 'doppelganger' bird is to show this change visually: the height of the illustration has been adjusted proportionately to reflect the decline. Of course, in some cases the smaller images are barely visible – most notably for the likes of Lesser Spotted Woodpecker, Turtle Dove and Willow Tit – but if you look long and hard, you might be able to spot them. It's rather like being in the in countryside.

For five species where no percentage change figure is available in the government report, I have used the British Trust for Ornithology Breeding Atlas (1976 edition), compared against the most recent RSPB population estimate to arrive at a value.

While this is a simplistic approach, and by definition every figure is an estimate, there is a consistency at the trend level that is compelling.

(And there are my log books.)

UK Government report: Department for Environment, Food & Rural Affairs – *Wild Bird Populations in the UK, 1970-2019*

https://assets.publishing.service.gov.uk/government/uploads/system/uploads/attachment_data/file/1039187/UK_Wild_birds_1970-2020_FINAL.pdf

The Atlas of Breeding Birds in Britain and Ireland, British Trust for Ornithology/Irish Wildbird Conservancy, T&AD Poyser (1976)

The RSPB website
https://www.rspb.org.uk

ABOUT THE AUTHOR

Cattle Egret ahoy, July 1971

Ian Moore is an award-wining writer and a member of the Society of Authors. A lifelong naturalist, he has watched birds in more than 60 countries, identifying over 1,000 species. His passion, however, has been the systematic observation of his 'local patch', beginning in the English Midlands in 1970 – a project that is presently settled in Edinburgh. As a teenager he was Field Officer of Hinckley & District Natural History Society. He studied Zoology at St Andrews University on the Fife coast, and worked as Assistant Warden at Holme Bird Observatory in Norfolk. He is the author of *I-SPY Scottish Nature* (Michelin 2011) and presently conducts guided walks and gives talks in his voluntary capacity as Wildlife Liaison Officer for Friends of Corstorphine Hill, a 200-acre nature reserve located in the Scottish capital's western suburbs.

*

Net royalties from the sale of this book will be divided equally between Burbage Junior School (nature projects), the Norfolk Ornithologists' Association, and Friends of Corstorphine Hill.

INDEX

A

Adrian Bawdon 88
Agrochemical industry 119
Aquatic Warbler 88
Arctic Warbler 88
Ashby-de-la-Zouch canal 57
Ash-Pole Spinney 51, 58, 120
Avocet 117

B

Badger 62-63, 108
Baird's Sandpiper 89
Bank Vole 49
Barred Warbler 88
Barn Owl 48, **49**, 54, 63, 72, 75, 91, 120
Barn Owl diet 49
BBC Winterwatch 122
Bean Goose 89
Blackcap 60, 68, 76, 90, 106, 111, 118
Blue-winged Teal 89
Bill Booth 56
Billy Bishop 81
Bird Life 14
Bittern 117

Blackbird 21, 38, **39**, 48, 55, 68, 71, 75, 105, 122
Black-headed Gull 37, 48, 70, 74
Black Redstart 30, 76
Black-tailed Godwit 117
Bluebells 59
Blue Tit 22, 43, 68, 71, 76, 107
Brambling 61, 77, 106
Brancaster Common 90
Broad-billed Sandpiper 89
British Trust for Ornithology 49, 130
Bullfinch 22, **40**, 69, 71, 77, 105
Bullfurlong Lane 16, 44, 47
Bullhead 49
Burbage 13, 16
Burbage church 26, 28
Burbage Junior School 14
Buzzard 64, 74, 104, 107, 117

C

Campendium 93, 98
Canada Goose 57, 67, 74
Carrion Crow 24, 68, 72, 76, 107, 118
Cattle Egret 87
Cetti's Warbler 88, 118
Chaffinch 21, 22, 43, 61, 69, 71, 77, 90
Chiffchaff 60, 63, 76, 106, 111, 118
Chilloutdoors blog 103
Chough 117
Cirl Bunting 117

Cley Marshes 19, 78, 81
Coal Tit 43, 76
Collared Dove 48, 68, 75, 112
Common Agricultural Policy 118, 122
Common Carp 56
Common Gull 37, 70, 75
Common Shrew 40, 49
Common Snipe **25**, 53, 70, 74
Coot 54, 57, 67, 74
Cormorant **58**, 73
Corn Bunting 34, **35**, 53, 77, 91, 95, 120
Corncrake 117
Corstorphine Hill LNR 103, 126
Crab-Tree Spinney 51, **62**, 126
Crane 89, 117
Crossbill 106, 112
Cross Roads Farm 31, 36, 39, 44
Cuckoo 23, 28, **29**, 40, 51, 68, 75, 90, 96, 120

D

Dartford Warbler 117
DDT 118
Dipper 104, 111
Dotterel 89
drift migrant 29
Dunnock 21, **43**, 69, 71, 77, 105, 107, 111
Dutch elm disease 27, 119, 122

E

Elm (tree) 27, 45
ELMS 124-125
Eye Brook Reservoir 19, 78

F

Fan-tailed Warbler 82, 87, 88, 92, 94
Fieldfare 23, 39, 47, 71, 75, 112
Fields south of Coventry Road 16, 19, **43**
Foster's Pond 16, 19, **48**, 56

G

Gadwall 57, 73
Garden Warbler **51**, 60, 63, 69, 76, 90, 97, 121
Garganey 89
George Eliot 15
Ghost Swift 27
Goldcrest 30, **31**, 46, 69, 71, 76, 87, 106, 112
Golden Oriole 93
Golden Plover 48, 74
Goldfinch 13, 21, 22, 32, 47, 69, 71, 77, 118
Goosander 104, 111
Graham Parker 51, 82 , 85, 88
Grasshopper Warbler 41, **42**, 52, 76, 96, 120
Great Black-backed Gull 37, **38**, 74
Great Bustard 117
Great Crested Grebe **57**, 73
Great Crested Newt 14

Great Grey Shrike **65-66**, 71, 77, 93
Great Spotted Woodpecker 27, 52, 70, 75, 106, 107, 111, 118
Great Tit 22, 43, 68, 71, 76, 107, 118
Greenfinch 21, 22, 33, **34**, 47, 69, 71, 77, 105, 107
Greenland Wheatear 93
Greenish Warbler 86, 88
Green Sandpiper 53, 74
Green Woodpecker 90, 113, 123
Grey Heron **25**, 57, 67, 73, 104, 112
Grey Partridge 35, **36**, 48, 59, 74, 90
Grey Phalarope 89
Grey Wagtail **36**, 104, 112
Gyrfalcon 87

H

Harlequin Duck 87
Hawfinch 113
hedgerow 45-46, 55, 104-5, 119, 120, 125
Herring Gull 37, **38**, 70, 75
Hinckley 13, 15
Hinckley & District Natural History Society
Holme Bird Observatory 81, 86, 91, 96, 97
Honey Buzzard 91
Hoopoe 93
House Martin 25, **26**, 75, 106, 112
House Sparrow 21, 22, **23**, 33, 47, 69, 71, 77, 111

I

Icterine Warbler 88
Isle of Man 21

J

Jackdaw 43, 68, 76, 104, 106, 107, 109, 118
Jack Reynolds 84
Jack Snipe 53, 74
Jay 55, 60, 72, 76, 95, 112
John Campton 51, 82, 85, 88, 94
John Foster 56

K

Ken Hill Wood 90, 95, 126
Ken Loach 32
Kentish Plover 89
Kes 32
Kestrel **32**, 33, 40, 67, 70, 74, 104, 107, 112, 113
Kingfisher **62**, 75, 104

L

Lapwing **37**, 48, 67, 70, 74
Leicester Grange 56
Leicestershire 15, 17
Lesser Black-backed Gull 37, 74
Lesser Redpoll **55**, 69, 71, 77, 90, 96, 106, 112
Lesser Spotted Woodpecker **27**, 52, 75, 90, 95, 121

Lesser Whitethroat 30, 76, 90, 96, 97
Linnet 13, 21, **33**, 47, 69, 71, 77, 90, 113, 120
Little Auk 86
Little Egret 118
Little Grebe **58**, 73
Little Owl 49, **50**, 75, 91
local patch 13, 91
log book 20, 21
Long-eared Owl 85, 90
Long-tailed Skua 89
Long-tailed Tit 46, 71, 76, 87, 107, 112, 118
Lord Melchett 85, 99

M

M69 17
Magpie 22, 43, 68, 72, 76, 118
Mallard 54, 57, 67, 70, 73, 104, 111, 118
marsh 50-51
Marsh Harrier 96
Marsh Sandpiper 89
Marsh Tit **31**, 68, 71, 76, 95
Meadow Brown 46
Meadow Pipit 21, 36, **37**, 70, 77, 112
Mediterranean Gull 81
Merlin 64, 74, 104
Middlemarch 15, 17, 20, 23, 126
Mistle Thrush 22, **38**, 48, 68, 75, 99, 107, 110, 112
Mitchell's Rule 107
Moorhen 44, **45**, 55, 57, 67, 74, 104, 111

moth trap 51
Mute Swan 57, 74, 104

N

Nancy's Café, Cley 86
Natterer's Bat 108
natural selection 9
Nightingale 90, 95
Nightjar 18, 90, 95
Norfolk Ornithologists' Association 81, 97
Nuneaton 15
Nuthatch 107, 111, 118

O

Osprey 104, 111, 117
Outwoods 14

P

Pallas's Sandgrouse 19
Pallas's Warbler 88, 92
Palmate Newt 108
Pectoral Sandpiper 89
Peregrine 104, 117
Peter Clarke 81, 85, **91-92**, 97
Pheasant 45, 59, 67, 74, 113
Pied Flycatcher **30**, 76, 93, 96, 97
Pied Wagtail 35, 36, 47, 57, 69, 71, 77, 113
Pink-footed Goose 111

Pochard 57, 70, 74
ponds 61-62
population, England 122
population, Scotland 122
Pyeharps 39, 41

Q

Quail 91

R

Raven 104, 111
Record's Pond 44
Red-backed Shrike 18, 90
Red Kite 104, 117
Red-legged Partridge 59, 74
Red-necked Phalarope 87, 89
Redstart 29, 76, 90, 93, 96, 97, 112
Redwing 39, 47, 71, 75, 87, 105, 112
Reed Bunting 22, **34**, 47, 51, 69, 71, 77
Reginald Harrison 18
Richard Richardson 81, 85
Richard's Pipit 93
Ring-necked Parakeet 77
Ring Ouzel 90, 96
Ringstead Downs 90
Robin 14, 21, 41, 43, 68, 71, 76, 111
Rook 22, 35, 68, 72, 76, 113
Rough-legged Buzzard 86

Rowe's Farm 44, 48, 110
Royal Society for the Protection of Birds 117, 118, 119, 130

S

Sabine's Gull 89
Salmonberry 109
Salthouse Heath 90, 95, 126
Sand Martin 90
Savi's Warbler 88
Scaup 89
Sea Eagle 117
Sedge Warbler 41, **42**, 52, 76
Shorelark 93
Short-eared Owl 50, 75, 96
Short-tailed Vole 40, 49
Shoveler 57, 74
Siskin 55, 77, 106, 112
Sketchley Road 16, 41
Skylark 13, 21, **35**, 36, 40, 52, 68, 70, 75, 112
Snow Bunting 93
Soar Brook 48, 49, 50, 56
Song Thrush 22, 38, **39**, 48, 68, 71, 75, 95, 105, 107
Sooty Shearwater 89
Sparrowhawk 64, 74, 104, 107, 117
splats 9, 126
Spoonbill 89
Spotted Crake 89
Spotted Flycatcher 9, **41**, 63, 76, 90, 93, 97, 106, 111, 113, 126

Starling 22, 27, **28**, 52, 69, 72, 73, 77, 106, 109, 111
Stock Dove 48, 59, 68, 70, 75, 90, 107, 109, 118, 120
Stonechat 30, 76
Stone Curlew 117
Stone Loach 49
Storm Petrel 86
Swallow 25, **26**, 41, 45, 68, 75, 106, 112
Swift 25, **26**, 68, 75, 106, 112

T

Tawny Owl 54, **55**, 60, 63, 75, 91, 104, 107, 120
Tawny Pipit 93
Teal 57, 70, 73
Ted Thornhill 18
Temminck's Stint
Three-Corner Spinney 50, 121
Three Pots 35
Thrush Nightingale 84
Treecreeper 60, **61**, 76, 107, 112
Tree Pipit **64**, 77, 93, 98
Tree Sparrow 13, 21, 22, **33**, 47, 52, 69, 72, 77, 90, 95, 96, 113, 120
Tufted Duck 55, 57, 74
Turtle Dove **46**, 51, 68, 75, 90, 91, 95, 96, 121
Twin Ponds 44, 87
Twite 93

U

Usual Area 16, 19, **23**

W

Warwickshire 15, 17
Water of Leith 104
Water Pipit 93
Water Rail 53, 70, 74
Watling Street 11, 16, 44
Waxwing 86
Wheatear 29, 64, 75, 96, 97, 112
Whimbrel 96
Whinchat **29**, 30, 64, 68, 76, 93, 96, 97
White-rumped Sandpiper 89
Whitethroat 40, 52, **53**, 69, 76, 90, 97, 106, 112
Wigeon 74
Willow Tit 22, **52**, 68, 71, 76, 95, 121
Willow Warbler 40, **52**, 63, 69, 76, 90, 97, 106, 112
Woodcock 53, **63**, 70, 74, 112, 121
Woodlark 18
Wood Mouse 49, 105
Woodpigeon 21, 43, 48, 68, 70, 75, 105, 106, 107, 118
Wood Warbler **60**, 76, 113
Wolvey 17
Wren 21, 43, 68, 71, 75, 111
Wryneck 93, 98

Y

Yellow-browed Warbler 88

Yellowhammer 13, **34**, 47, 69, 71, 77, 90, 111, 112
Yellow Wagtail 27, **28**, 29, 57, 69, 77, 93, 96, 120
YOC 14, 21, 85

Z

Zitting Cisticola 84

NOTES

Printed in Great Britain
by Amazon